# Finney On Revival

# Finney On Revival

*The Highlights
of the
Sermons on Revival*

*By
Charles Grandison Finney*

*Arranged by
E. E. Shelhamer*

**DIMENSION BOOKS**
BETHANY FELLOWSHIP, INC.
Minneapolis, Minn. 55438

*ISBN 0-87123-151-4*
*DIMENSION BOOKS*
*are published by*
*Bethany Fellowship, Inc.*
*6820 Auto Club Road*
*Minneapolis, Minnesota 55438*

Printed in U.S.A.

# PREFACE

THE lectures of Charles Grandison Finney on *Revivals of Religion* constitute probably the most exhaustive treatment of the subject that can be found. The lectures were the result of intense study, both of the Bible and of human need, by a man of lofty spirituality and distinguished as evangelist, pastor and theologian.

He was pre-eminently the nineteenth-century apostle of Revival. It is estimated that over 250,000 souls were converted as the result of his preaching.

In these busy days it is frequently claimed that there is little time for the study of the larger works which have contained his messages. In this new book, however, an attempt has been made to gather the main points from the large amount of material available, in order to provide a handbook for those Christian workers who would learn the simple principles which govern the promise of Revival.

It is taken for granted that God's blessing will come in His own way and in His own good time, but Finney shows that the Scriptures have made it plain that blessing follows when certain conditions are fulfilled in the hearts and lives of men. The essentials are set forth in these pages in Finney's own words, that he may speak to this generation to encourage and inspire all who look for Revival in our own time.

E. E. S.

# CONTENTS

# Finney On Revival

## CHAPTER I

### HOW TO BEGIN A REVIVAL

#### What is a Revival?

A REVIVAL is nothing else than a new beginning of obedience to God. Just as in the case of a converted sinner, the first step is a deep repentance, a breaking down of heart, a getting down into the dust before God, with deep humility, and a forsaking of sin.

An individual once went into a manufactory to see the machinery. (This was Mr. Finney himself.) His mind was solemn, as he had been where there was a revival. The people who laboured there all knew him by sight, and knew who he was. A young lady who was at work saw him and whispered some foolish remark to her companion, and laughed. The person stopped and looked at her with a feeling of grief. She stopped; her thread broke —and then she was so much agitated that she could not join it. She looked out at the window to compose herself, and then tried again; again and again she strove to recover her self-command. At length she sat down, overcome by her feelings. The person then approached and spoke with her; she soon manifested a deep sense of sin. The feeling spread through the establishment like fire, and in a few hours almost every person employed there was under conviction; so much so that the owner, though a worldly man, was astounded, and requested to have the works stopped and a prayer-meeting held; for, he said, it was a great deal more important to have these people converted than to have the works go on. And in a few days the owner and nearly all the persons employed in the establishment (about 3,000) were hopefully converted. The eye of this individual, his solemn countenance, his compassionate feeling, rebuked the levity of the young woman, and brought her under conviction of sin; and probably in a great measure this whole revival followed from so small an incident.

# CHAPTER II

## WHEN TO EXPECT A REVIVAL

*"Wilt not Thou revive us again, that Thy people may rejoice in Thee?"*—Psalm lxxxv. 6.

1. WHEN there is a want of brotherly love and Christian confidence among professors of religion, then a revival is needed. Then there is a loud call for God to revive His work.

2. When there are dissensions, and jealousies, and evil speakings among professors of religion, then there is a great need of a revival. These things show that Christians have got far from God, and it is time to think earnestly of a revival.

3. When there is a worldly spirit in the Church. It is manifest that the Church has sunk down into a low and back-slidden state, when you see Christians conform to the world in dress, equipage, and "parties," in seeking worldly amusements, and reading novels, and other books such as the world reads.

4. When the Church finds its members falling into gross and scandalous sins, then it is time to awake and cry to God for a revival of religion.

5. When sinners are careless and stupid, it is time Christians should bestir themselves. It is as much their duty to awake as it is for the firemen to do so when a fire breaks out in the night in a great city. The Church ought to put out the fires of hell which are laying hold of the wicked. Sleep! Should the firemen sleep and let the whole city burn down, what would be thought of such firemen? And yet their guilt would not compare with the guilt of

Christians who sleep while sinners around them are sinking stupidly into the fires of hell.

6. If a minister finds he has lost in any degree the confidence of his people, he ought to labour for a revival as the only means of regaining their confidence. I do not mean that his motive should be merely to regain the confidence of his people, but that a revival through his instrumentality (and ordinarily nothing else) will restore to him the confidence of the praying part of his people. So if an elder or private member of the Church finds his brethren cold towards him, there is but one way to restore it. It is by being revived himself, and pouring out from his eyes and from his life the splendour of the image of Christ.

The fact is, Christians are more to blame for not being revived than sinners are for not being converted.

7. A Church declining in this way cannot continue to exist without a revival. If it receives new members, they will, for the most part, be made up of ungodly persons. Without revivals there will not ordinarily be as many persons converted as will die off in a year. There have been Churches in this country where the members have died off, and, since there were no revivals to convert others in their place, the Church has "run out," and the organisation has been dissolved.

8. Without a revival sinners will grow harder and harder under preaching, and will experience a more horrible damnation than they would if they had never heard the Gospel. Your children and your friends will go down to a much more horrible fate in hell, in consequence of the means of grace, if there are no revivals to convert them to God. Better were it for them if there were no means of grace, no sanctuary, no Bible, no preaching, than to live and die where there is no revival. The Gospel is the savour of death unto death, if it is not made a savour of life unto life.

9. There is no other way in which a Church can be sanctified, grow in grace, and be fitted for heaven. What is "growing in grace"? Is it hearing sermons and getting some new notions about religion? No; no such thing. The Christian who does this, and nothing more, is getting worse and worse, more and more hardened, and every week it is more difficult to rouse him up to duty.

10. A revival may be expected when Christians have a spirit of prayer for a revival. That is, when they pray as if their hearts were set upon it. Sometimes Christians are not engaged in definite prayer for a revival, not even when they are warm in prayer. Their minds are upon something else; they are praying for something else—the salvation of the heathen and the like—and not for a revival among themselves. But when they feel the want of a revival, they pray for it; they feel for their own families and neighbourhoods; they pray for them as if they could not be denied.

What constitutes a spirit of prayer? Is it many prayers and warm words? No. Prayer is the state of the heart. The spirit of prayer is a state of continual desire and anxiety of mind for the salvation of sinners. It is something that weighs them down. It is the same, so far as the philosophy of mind is concerned, as when a man is anxious for some wordly interest. A Christian who has this spirit of prayer feels anxious for souls. It is the subject of his thoughts all the time, and makes him look and act as if he had a load on his mind. He thinks of it by day, and dreams of it by night. This is properly "praying without ceasing." His prayers seem to flow from his heart liquid as water: "O Lord, revive Thy work." Sometimes this feeling is very deep; persons have been bowed down so that they could neither stand nor sit.

11. This is by no means enthusiasm. It is just what Paul felt when he said: "My little children, of whom I

travail in birth." This travail of soul is that deep agony which persons feel when they lay hold on God for such a blessing, and will not let Him go till they receive it. I do not mean to be understood that it is essential to a spirit of prayer that the distress should be so great as this. But this deep, continual, earnest desire for the salvation of sinners is what constitutes the spirit of prayer for a revival.

12. When this feeling exists in a Church, unless the Spirit is grieved away by sin, there will infallibly be a revival of Christians generally, and it will involve the conversion of sinners to God. A clergyman once told me of a revival among his people, which commenced with a zealous and devoted woman in the Church. She became anxious about sinners, and gave herself to praying for them; she prayed, and her distress increased; and she finally came to her minister and talked with him, asking him to appoint an anxious inquirers' meeting, for she felt that one was needed. The minister put her off, for he felt nothing of any such need. The next week she came again, and besought him again to appoint such a meeting. She knew there would be somebody to come, for she felt as if God was going to pour out His Spirit. The minister once more put her off.

And finally she said to him: "If you do not appoint the meeting I shall die, for there is certainly going to be a revival." The next Sabbath he appointed a meeting, and said that if there were any who wished to converse with him about the salvation of their souls, he would meet them on such an evening. He did not know of one, but when he went to the place, to his astonishment he found a large number of anxious inquirers. Now, do you not think that that woman knew there was going to be a revival? Call it what you please, a new revelation or an old revelation, or anything else. I say it was the Spirit of God that taught that praying woman there was going to be a revival. "The secret of the Lord" was with her, and she knew it. She knew God had been in her heart, and filled it so full that she could contain no longer.

13. A revival of religion may be expected when Christians begin to confess their sins to one another. At other times they confess in a general manner, as if they are only half in earnest. They may do it in eloquent language, but it does not mean anything. But when there is an ingenuous breaking down, and a pouring out of the heart in confession of sin, the flood-gates will soon burst open, and salvation will flow over the place.

14. A revival may be expected whenever Christians are found willing to make the sacrifices necessary to carry it on. They must be willing to sacrifice their feelings, their business, their time, to help forward the work. Ministers must be willing to lay out their strength, and to jeopard their health and life. They must be willing to offend the impenitent by plain and faithful dealing, and perhaps offend many members of the Church who will not come up to the work. They must take a decided stand with the revival, be the consequences what they may. They must be prepared to go on with the work even though they should lose the affections of all the impenitent, and of all the cold part of the Church. The minister must be prepared, if it be the will of God, to be driven away from the place. He must be determined to go straight forward, and leave the entire event with God.

15. I knew a minister who had a young man labouring with him in a revival. The young man preached pretty plain truth and the wicked did not like him. They said: "We like our minister and we wish to have him preach." They finally said so much that the minister told the young man: "Such and such a person, who gives so much towards

my support, says so-and-so; Mr. A. also says so, and Mr. B likewise. They think it will break up the society if you continue to preach, and I think you had better not preach any more." The young man went away, but the Spirit of God immediately withdrew from the place and the revival stopped short. The minister, by yielding to the wicked desires of the ungodly, drove Him away, being afraid that the devil would drive him away from his people. So by undertaking to satisfy the devil he offended God. And God so ordered events that in a short time the minister had to leave his people after all. He undertook to go between the devil and God, and God dismissed him.

# CHAPTER III

*"Break up your fallow ground : for it is time to seek the Lord,
till He come and rain righteousness upon you."*—Hosea x. 12.

THE Jews were a nation of farmers, and it is therefore a
common thing in the Scriptures to refer for illustrations
to their occupation, and to the scenes with which farmers
and shepherds are familiar. The prophet Hosea addresses
them as a nation of backsliders; he reproves them for
their idolatry, and threatens them with the judgments of
God.

A revival consists of two parts: as it respects the Church,
and as it respects the ungodly. I shall speak on this occasion
of a revival in the Church. Fallow ground is ground which
has once been tilled, but which now lies waste, and needs
to be broken up and mellowed, before it is suited to receive
grain.

If you mean to break up the fallow ground of your
hearts, you must begin by looking at your hearts: examine
and note the state of your minds, and see where you are.
Many never seem to think about this. They pay no attention
to their own hearts, and never know whether they are
doing well in religion or not; whether they are gaining
ground or going back; whether they are fruitful, or lying
waste. Now you must draw off your attention from other
things, and look into this. Make a business of it. Do not
be in a hurry. Examine thoroughly the state of your hearts,
and see where you are: whether you are walking with God
every day, or with the devil.

Self-examination consists in looking at your lives, in

17

considering your actions, in calling up the past, and learning
its true character. Look back over your past history. Take
up your individual sins one by one, and look at them. I
do not mean that you should just cast a glance at your
past life, and see that it has been full of sins, and then go
to God and make a sort of general confession, and ask for
pardon. That is not the way. You must take them up one
by one. It will be a good thing to take a pen and paper,
as you go over them, and write them down as they occur
to you.

Go over them as carefully as a merchant goes over his
books; and as often as a sin comes before your memory,
add it to the list. General confessions of sin will never
do. Your sins were committed one by one; and as far
as you can come at them, they ought to be reviewed
and repented of one by one. Now begin, and take up
first what are commonly, but improperly, called Sins of
Omission.

1. *Ingratitude.* Take this sin, for instance, and write
down under that head all the instances you can remember
wherein you have received favours from God for which
you have never exercised gratitude. How many cases
can you remember? Some remarkable providence, some
wonderful turn of events, that saved you from ruin. Set
down the instances of God's goodness to you when you
were in sin, before your conversion, for which you have
never been half thankful enough; and the numerous mercies
you have received since. How long the catalogue of instances,
where your ingratitude has been so black that you are forced
to hide your face in confusion! Go on your knees and
confess them one by one to God, and ask forgiveness. The
very act of confession, by the laws of suggestion, will
bring up others to your memory. Put down these! Go
over them three or four times in this way, and see what an

astonishing number of mercies there are for which you have never thanked God.

2. *Want of love to God.* Think how grieved and alarmed you would be if you discovered any flagging of affection for you in your wife, husband, or children; if you saw another engrossing their hearts, and thoughts, and time. Perhaps in such a case you would wellnigh die with a just and virtuous jealousy. Now, God calls Himself a jealous God; and have you not given your heart to other loves and infinitely offended Him?

3. *Neglect of the Bible.* Put down the cases when for perhaps weeks, or longer, God's Word was not a pleasure. Some people, indeed, read over whole chapters in such a way that they could not tell what they had been reading. If so, no wonder that your life is spent at random, and that your religion is such a miserable failure.

4. *Unbelief.* Recall the instances in which you have virtually charged the God of truth with lying, by your unbelief of His express promises and declarations. God has promised to give the Holy Spirit to them that ask Him. Now, have you believed this? Have you expected Him to answer? Have you not virtually said in your hearts, when you prayed for the Holy Spirit: "I do not believe that I shall receive"? If you have not believed nor expected to receive the blessing which God has expressly promised, you have charged Him with lying.

5. *Neglect of prayer.* Think of the times when you have neglected secret prayer, family prayer, and prayer-meetings; or have prayed in such a way as more grievously to offend God than to have omitted it altogether.

6. *Neglect of the means of grace.* When you have suffered trifling excuses to prevent your attending meetings, have neglected and poured contempt upon the means of salvation, merely from disrelish of spiritual duties.

7. *The manner in which you have performed those duties.* That is, with want of feeling and want of faith, in a worldly frame of mind, so that your words were nothing but a mere chattering of a wretch who did not deserve that God should feel the least care for him. When you have fallen down upon your knees and "said your prayers" in such an un-feeling and careless manner that if you had been put under oath five minutes after you could not have said for what you had been praying.

8. *Want of love for the souls of your fellow-men.* Look round upon your friends and relatives, and remember how little compassion you have felt for them. You have stood by and seen them going right to hell, and it seems as though you did not care. How many days have there been, in which you failed to make their condition the subject of a single fervent prayer, or to evince any ardent desire for their salvation?

9. *Want of care for the heathen.* Perhaps you have not cared enough for them to attempt to learn their condition; perhaps not even to take a missionary magazine. Look at this, and see how much you really care for the heathen, and set down honestly the real amount of your feelings for them, and your desire for their salvation. Measure your desire for their salvation. Measure your desire for their salvation by the self-denial you practice, in giving of your substance to send them the Gospel. Do you deny yourself even the hurtful superfluities of life, such as tea, coffee, and tobacco? Do you retrench your style of living, and scruple not to subject yourself to any inconvenience to save them? Do you daily pray for them in private? Are you laying by something to put into the treasury of the Lord when you go up to pray? If you are not doing these things, and if your soul is not agonised for the poor benighted heathen, why are you such a hypocrite as to pretend to

be a Christian? Why, your profession is an insult to Jesus Christ!

10. *Neglect of family duties.* Think of how you have lived before your family, how you have prayed, what an example you have set before them. What direct efforts do you habitually make for their spiritual good? What duty have you *not* neglected?

11. *Neglect of watchfulness over your own life.* In how many instances you have hurried over your private duties, and have neither taken yourself to task, nor honestly made up your accounts with God; how often have you entirely neglected to watch your conduct, and, having been off your guard, have sinned before the world, and before the Church, and before God!

12. *Neglect to watch over your brethren.* How often have you broken your covenant that you would watch over them in the Lord? How little do you know or care about the state of their souls? And yet you are under a solemn duty to watch over them. What have you done to make yourself acquainted with them? In how many of them have you interested yourself, to know their spiritual state? Go over the list, and wherever you find there has been a neglect, write it down. How many times have you seen your brethren growing cold in religion, and have not spoken to them about it? You have seen them beginning to neglect one duty after another, and you did not reprove them, in a brotherly way. You have seen them falling into sin, and you let them go on. And yet you pretend to love them. What a hypocrite! Would you see your wife or child going into disgrace, or falling into the fire, and hold your peace? No, you would not. What do you think of yourself, then, to pretend to love Christians (and to love Christ) while you see them going into disgrace, and yet say nothing to them?

13. *Neglect of self-denial.* There are many professors who are willing to do almost anything in religion, that does not require self-denial. But when they are required to do anything that requires them to deny themselves—oh, that is too much! They think they are doing a great deal for God, and doing about as much as He ought in reason to ask, if they are only doing what they can do just as well as not; but they are not willing to deny themselves any comfort or convenience whatever for the sake of serving the Lord. They will not willingly suffer reproach for the name of Christ. Nor will they deny themselves the luxuries of life, to save a world from hell. So far are they from remembering that self-denial is a condition of discipleship that they do not know what self-denial is. They never have really denied themselves a riband or a pin for Christ and the Gospel. Oh, how soon such professors will be in hell! Some are giving of their abundance, and are giving much, and are ready to complain that others do not give more; when, in truth, they do not themselves give anything that they need, anything that they could enjoy if they kept it. They only give of their surplus wealth; and perhaps that poor woman who puts in her mite has exercised more self-denial than they have in giving thousands.

From these we now turn to Sins of Commission.

14. *Worldly mindedness.* What has been the state of your heart in regard to your worldly possessions? Have you looked at them as really yours—as if you had a right to dispose of them as your own, according to your own will? If you have, write that down. If you have loved property, and sought after it for its own sake, or to gratify lust or ambition, or a worldly spirit, or to lay it up for your families, you have sinned, and must repent.

15. *Pride.* Recollect all the instances you can, in which you have detected yourself in the exercise of pride. Vanity

is a particular form of pride. How many times have you detected yourself in consulting vanity about your dress and appearance? How many times have you thought more, and taken more pains, and spent more time about decorating your body to go to Church, than you have about preparing your mind for the worship of God? You have gone caring more as to how you appeared outwardly, in the sight of mortal man, than how your soul appeared in the sight of the heart-searching God. You have, in fact, set up yourself to be worshipped by them, rather than prepared to worship God yourself. You sought to divide the worship of God's house, to draw off the attention of God's people to look at your pretty appearance. It is in vain to pretend, now, that you do not care anything about having people look at you. Be honest about it! Would you take all this pain about your looks if every person were blind?

16. *Envy.* Look at the cases in which you were envious of those whom you thought were above you in any respect. Or perhaps you have envied those who have been more talented or more useful than yourself. Have you not so envied some, that you have been pained to hear them praised? It has been more agreeable to you to dwell upon their faults than upon their virtues, upon their failures than upon their successes. Be honest with yourself; and if you have harboured this spirit of hell, repent deeply before God, or He will never forgive you.

17. *Censoriousness.* Instances in which you have had a bitter spirit, and spoken of Christians in a manner devoid of charity and love; or charity, which requires you always to hope the best the case will admit, and to put the best construction upon any ambiguous conduct.

18. *Slander.* The times you have spoken behind people's backs of the faults, real or supposed, of members of the Church or others, unnecessarily, or without good reason.

This is slander. You need not lie to be guilty of slander: to tell the truth with the design to injure is slander.

19. *Levity.* How often have you trifled before God as you would not have dared to trifle in the presence of an earthly sovereign? You have either been an atheist, and forgotten that there was a God, or have had less respect for Him, and His presence, than you would have had for an earthly judge.

20. *Lying.* Understand now what lying is. Any species of designed deception. If the deception be not designed, it is not lying. But if you design to make an impression contrary to the naked truth, you lie. Put down all those cases you can recollect. Do not call them by any soft names. God calls them LIES, and charges you with LYING, and you had better charge yourself correctly. How innumerable are the falsehoods perpetuated every day in business, and in social intercourse, by words, and looks, and actions, designed to make an impression on others, for selfish reasons that are contrary to the truth!

21. *Cheating.* Set down all the cases in which you have dealt with an individual, and done to him that which you would not like to have done to you. That is cheating. God has laid down a rule in the case: "All things whatsoever ye would that men should do to you, do ye even so to them." That is the rule. And if you have not done so you are a cheat. Mind, the rule is not that you should do "what you might reasonably expect them to do to you", for that is a rule which would admit of every degree of wickedness. But it is: "As ye WOULD they should do to you."

22. *Hypocrisy.* For instance, in your prayers and confessions to God. Set down the instances in which you have prayed for things you did not really want. And the evidence is, that when you have done praying, you could

not tell for what you had prayed. How many times have you confessed sins that you did not mean to break off, and when you had no solemn purpose not to repeat them? Yes, have confessed sins when you knew you as much expected to go and repeat them, as you expected to live.

23. *Robbing God.* Think of the instances in which you have misspent your time, squandering the hours which God gave you to serve Him and save souls, in vain amusements or foolish conversation, in reading novels or doing nothing; cases where you have misapplied your talents and powers of mind; where you have squandered money on your lusts, or spent it for things which you did not need, and which did not contribute to your health, comfort, or usefulness. Perhaps some of you have laid out God's money for tobacco. I will not speak of intoxicating drink, for I presume there is no professor of religion here that would drink it; and I hope there is not one that uses that filthy poison, tobacco. Think of a professor of religion using God's money to poison himself with tobacco!

24. *Bad Temper.* Perhaps you have abused your wife, or your children, or your family, or servants, or neighbours. Write it all down.

25. *Hindering others from being useful.* Perhaps you have weakened their influence by insinuations against them. You have not only robbed God of your own talents, but tied the hands of somebody else. What a wicked servant is he who not only loiters himself but hinders the rest! This is done sometimes by taking their time needlessly; sometimes by destroying Christian confidence in them. Thus you have played into the hands of Satan, and not only showed yourself an idle vagabond, but prevented others from working.

If you find you have committed a fault against an individual, and that individual is within your reach, go and confess it immediately, and get that out of the way. If the individual you have injured is too far off for you to go and see him, sit down and write him a letter confessing the injury. If you have defrauded anybody, send the money, the full amount and the interest.

Go thoroughly to work in all this! Go now! Do not put it off; that will only make the matter worse. Confess to God those sins that have been committed against God, and to man, those sins that have been committed against man. Do not think of getting off by going round the stumbling-blocks. Take them up out of the way. In breaking up your fallow ground, you must remove every obstruction. Things may be left that you think little things, and you may wonder why you do not feel as you wish to feel in religion, when the reason is that your proud and carnal mind has covered up something which God required you to confess and remove. Break up all the ground and turn it over. Do not "Balk" it, as the farmers say; do not turn aside for little difficulties; drive the plough right through them, beam deep, and turn the ground up, so that it may all be mellow and soft, and fit to receive the seed and bear fruit "an hundredfold."

26. When you have gone over your whole history in this way, thoroughly, if you will then go over the ground the second time, and give your solemn and fixed attention to it, you will find that the things you have put down will suggest other things of which you have been guilty, connected with them, or near them. Then go over it a third time, and you will recollect other things connected with these. And you will find in the end that you can remember an amount of history, and particular actions, even in this life, which you did not think you would remember in eternity. Unless you take up your sins in this way, and consider them in detail, one by one, you can form no idea

of the amount of them. You should go over the list as thoroughly, and as carefully, and as solemnly, as you would if you were just preparing yourself for the Judgment.

As you go over the catalogue of your sins, be sure to resolve upon present and *entire* reformation. Wherever you find anything wrong, resolve at once, *in the strength of God, to sin no more in that way.* It will be of no benefit to examine yourself, unless you determine to amend in every particular that which you find wrong in heart, temper, or conduct.

If you find, as you go on with this duty, that your mind is still all dark, cast about you, and you will find there is some reason for the Spirit of God to depart from you. You have not been faithful and thorough. In the progress of such a work you have got to do violence to yourself and bring yourself as a rational being up to this work, with the Bible before you, and try your heart till you *do* feel. You need not expect that God will work a miracle for you to break up your fallow ground. It is to be done by means. Fasten your attention to the subject of your sins. You cannot look at your sins long and thoroughly and see how bad they are, without feeling and feeling deeply.

Experience fully proves the benefit of going over our history in this way. Set yourself to the work now; resolve that you will never stop till you find you can pray. You never will have the Spirit of God dwelling in you till you have unravelled this whole mystery of iniquity, and spread out your sins before God. Let there be this deep work of repentance and full confession, this breaking down before God, and you will have as much of the spirit of prayer as your body can bear up under. The reason why so few Christians know anything about the spirit of prayer is because they never would take the pains to examine themselves properly, and so never knew what it was to have their hearts all broken up in this way.

27. It will do no good to preach to you while your hearts are in this hardened, and waste, and fallow state. The farmer might just as well sow his grain on the rock. It will bring forth no fruit. This is the reason why there are so many fruitless professors in the Church, and why there is so much outside machinery and so little deep-toned feeling. Look at the Sabbath-school, for instance, and see how much machinery there is and how little of the power of godliness. If you go on in this way the Work of God will continue to harden you, and you will grow worse and worse, just as the rain and snow on an old fallow field make the turf thicker and the clods stronger.

28. Professors of religion should never satisfy themselves, or expect a revival, just by starting out of their slumbers, and blustering about, and talking to sinners. They must get their fallow ground broken up. It is utterly unphilo-sophical to think of getting engaged in religion in this way. If your fallow ground is broken up, then the way to get more feeling is to go out and see sinners on the road to hell, and talk to them, and guide inquiring souls. Then you will get more feeling. You may get into an excitement without this breaking up; you may show a kind of zeal, but it will not last long, and it will not take hold of sinners, unless your hearts are broken up. The reason is, that you go about mechanically, and have not broken up your fallow ground.

29. And now, finally, will you break up your fallow ground? Will you enter upon the course now pointed out and persevere till you are thoroughly awake? If you fail here, if you do not do this, and get prepared, you can go no farther with me. I have gone with you as far as it is of any use to go until your fallow ground is broken up.

Now, you must make thorough work upon this point, or all I have further to say will do you little good. Nay, it will only harden, and make you worse. If you do not set about this work immediately I shall take it for granted that you do not mean to be revived, that you have forsaken your minister, and mean to let him go up to battle alone. If you do not do this, I charge you with having forsaken Christ, with refusing to repent and do your first works.

# CHAPTER IV

## THE SPIRIT OF PRAYER

*"Likewise the Spirit also helpeth our infirmities: for we know not what we should pray for as we ought: but the Spirit itself maketh intercession for us with groanings which cannot be uttered.*

*And He that searcheth the hearts knoweth what is the mind of the Spirit, because He maketh intercession for the saints according to the will of God."*—Romans viii. 26, 27.

WE are so ignorant both of the will of God, revealed in the Bible, and of His unrevealed will, as we ought to learn it from His providence. Mankind is vastly ignorant both of the promises and prophesies of the Bible, and blind to the providence of God. And they are still more in the dark about those points of which God has said nothing but through the leadings of His Spirit. I have named these four sources of evidence on which to ground faith in prayer—*promises, prophecies, providences,* and the *Holy Spirit.* When all other means fail of leading us to the knowledge of what we ought to pray for, the Spirit does it.

I once knew an individual (doubtless he meant himself) who was in great spiritual darkness. He had retired for prayer, resolved that he would not desist till he had found the Lord. He kneeled down and tried to pray. All was dark, and he could not pray. He rose from his knees, and stood awhile; but he could not give it up, for he had promised that he would not let the sun go down before he had given himself to God. He knelt again; but all was dark, and his heart was as hard as before. He was nearly in despair, and said in agony: "I have grieved the Spirit of God away, and there is no promise for me. I am shut out from the presence of God."

But his resolution was formed not to give over, and again he knelt down. He had said but a few words when this passage came into his mind, as fresh as if he had just read it: "Ye shall seek Me, and find Me, when ye shall search for Me with all your heart" (Jer. xxix. 13). He saw that though this promise was in the Old Testament, and addressed to the Jews, it was still as applicable to him as to them. And it broke his heart, like the hammer of the Lord, in a moment. And he prayed, and rose up happy in God.

(*Note.*—In this pathetic passage, Finney, adopting the Pauline "I knew a man" (2 Cor. xii. 2), gives the story of his own conversion. It was at Adams, N.Y., where he was studying law. He had been asked (in the prayer-meeting which he attended at the Presbyterian Church): "Do you not wish us to pray for you?" His rejoinder was characteristic, if irritable: "I do not see that it will do any good, for you are continually asking, but you do not receive. You have been praying for a revival of religion ever since I have been in Adams, and yet you have it not." Nevertheless, continuing his study of the Bible, he came under deepening conviction, realising that "salvation, instead of being a thing to be wrought out by my own works, was a thing to be found entirely in the Lord Christ, who presented Himself as my God and my Saviour." As he walked along the street, an inward voice seemed to demand of him: "Will you accept it now, to-day?" and his reply was: "Yes, I will accept it to-day, or I will die in the attempt."

Instead of proceeding to his studies he made his way into a wood near the village, and crept between some fallen trees, to pray. There, as he afterwards said: "God gave me many other promises" (in addition to the text quoted from Jeremiah), "especially some most precious promises respecting our Lord Jesus Christ. I seized hold of them." His perturbed mind became "most wonderfully calm and peaceful"; indeed, as he walked back towards Adams "so perfectly quiet was my mind that it seemed as if all nature listened." He had gone to the woods immediately after an early breakfast, and now it was dinner-time, yet it appeared to him that he had been absent but a little while.)

I was acquainted with an individual (Rev. Daniel Nash), who used to keep a list of persons for whom he was especially concerned; and I have had the opportunity to know a multitude of persons, for whom he became thus interested, who were immediately converted. I have seen him pray for persons on his list when he was literally in an agony for them; and have sometimes known him call on some other person to help him pray for such-a-one. I have known his mind to fasten thus on an individual of hardened, abandoned character, and who could not be reached in any ordinary way.

In a town in a northern part of this State, where there was a revival, there was a certain individual who was a most violent and outrageous opposer. He kept a tavern and used to delight in swearing at a desperate rate, whenever there were Christians within hearing, on purpose to hurt their feelings. He was so bad that one man said he believed he should have to sell his place, or give it away, and move from the town, for he could not live near a man who swore so. This good man of whom I am speaking passed through the town, and, hearing of the case, was very much grieved and distressed for the individual. He took him on his praying list. The case weighed on his mind when he was asleep and when he was awake. He kept thinking about the ungodly man, and praying for him, for days. And, the first we knew of it, the tavern-keeper came into a meeting, got up and confessed his sins, and poured out his soul—one of the most heartbroken I ever heard. It seemed to cover the whole ground of his treatment of God, of Christians, of the revival, and of everything good.

(*Note.*—In remarkable contrast was the case of a railing infidel who, in the midst of his opposition, was smitten with apoplexy. A physician assured him that he had not long to live, and that if he had anything to say he must say it at once. He had only time and strength to stammer out one sentence; it was: "Don't let Finney pray over my corpse.")

His bar-room immediately became the place where they held prayer-meetings. In this manner the Spirit of God leads individual Christians to pray for things which they would not pray for, unless they were led by the Spirit; and thus they pray for things "according to the will of God."

1. Great evil has been done by saying that this kind of influence amounts to a new revelation. Many people will be so afraid of it, if they hear it called a new revelation, that they will not stop to inquire what it means, or whether the Scriptures teach it or not. The plain truth of the matter is, that the Spirit leads a man to pray; and if God leads a man to pray for an individual, the inference from the Bible is, that God designs to save that individual. If we find, by comparing our state of mind with the Bible, that we are led by the Spirit to pray for an individual, we have good evidence to believe that God is prepared to bless him.

2. Devoted, praying Christians often see these things so clearly, and look so far ahead, as greatly to stumble others. They sometimes almost seem to prophesy. No doubt persons may be deluded, and sometimes are, by leaning to their own understanding when they think they are led by the Spirit. But there is no doubt that a Christian may be made to discern clearly the signs of the times, so as to understand, by Providence, what to expect, and thus to pray for it in faith. Thus they are often led to expect a revival, and to pray for it in faith, when nobody else can see the least sign of it.

3. There was a woman in New Jersey, in a place where there had been a revival. She was very positive there was going to be another. She wanted to have "conference meetings" appointed. But the minister and elders saw nothing to encourage it, and would do nothing. She saw they were blind, and so she went forward, and got a carpenter to make seats for her, for she said she would have meetings in her own house; there was certainly going to be a revival! She had scarcely opened her doors for meetings, before the

Spirit of God came down with great power, and these sleepy Church members found themselves surrounded all at once with convicted sinners. They could only say: "Surely the Lord is in this place; and we knew it not" (Gen. xxviii. 16). The reason why such persons as this praying woman understand the indication of God's will is not because of the superior wisdom that is in them, but because the Spirit of God leads them to see the signs of the times. And this, not by revelation; but they are led to see that converging of providences to a single point, which produces in them a confident expectation of a certain result.

The text says: "The Spirit maketh intercession with groanings that cannot be uttered." The meaning of this I understand to be, that the Spirit excites desires too great to be uttered except by groans—making the soul too full to utter its feelings by words, so that the person can only groan them out to God, who understands the language of the heart.

4. How is a sinner to get conviction? Why, by thinking of his sins. That is the way for a Christian to obtain deep feeling—by thinking upon the object. God is not going to pour these things on you without any effort of your own. You must cherish the slightest impressions. Take the Bible, and go over the passages that show the conditions and prospects of the world. Look at the world, look at your children, and your neighbours, and see their condition while they remain in sin; then, persevere in prayer and effort till you obtain the blessing of the Spirit of God.

I have dwelt the more on this subject, because I want to have it made so plain that you will be careful not to grieve the Spirit. I want you to have high ideas of the Holy Ghost, and to feel that nothing good will be done without His influences. No praying or preaching will be of any avail without Him. If Jesus Christ were to come down here and preach to sinners, not one would be converted without the Spirit. Be careful, then, not to grieve Him away, by slighting or neglecting His heavenly influences when He invites you to pray.

5. We see from this subject the absurdity of using set forms of prayer, or prayer books. The very idea of using a form rejects, of course, the leadings of the Spirit. Nothing is more calculated to destroy the spirit of prayer, and entirely to darken and confuse the mind, as to what constitutes prayer, than to use forms. Forms of prayer are not only absurd in themselves, but they are the very device of the devil to destroy the spirit and break the power of prayer. It is of no use to say the form is a good one. Prayer does not consist in words. And it matters not what the words are if the heart is not led by the Spirit of God. If the desire is not enkindled, the thoughts directed, and the whole current of feeling produced and led by the Spirit of God, it is not prayer. And set forms are, of all things, best calculated to keep an individual from praying as he ought.

6. "The Spirit maketh intercession"—for whom? For the saints! Those who are saints are thus exercised. If you are saints you know by experience what it is to be thus exercised; or, if you do not, it is because you have grieved the Spirit of God so that He will not lead you. You live in such a manner that this Holy Comforter will not dwell with you, nor give you the spirit of prayer. If this is so, you must repent. Do not stop to settle whether you are a Christian or not, but repent, as if you never had repented. Do your first works. Do not take it for granted that you are a Christian, but go, like a humble sinner, and pour out your heart unto the Lord. You never can have the spirit of prayer in any other way.

7. Nothing will produce an excitement and opposition so quickly as the spirit of prayer. If any person should feel

burdened with the case of sinners, so as to groan in his prayer, some become nervous, and he is visited at once with rebuke and opposition! From my soul I abhor all affectation of feeling where none exists, and all attempts to work one's self up into feeling, by groans. But I feel bound to defend the position, that there is such a thing as being in a state of mind in which there is but one way to keep from groaning; and that is, by resisting the Holy Ghost.

I was once present where this subject was discussed. It was said that "groaning ought to be discountenanced." The question was asked, in reply: Whether God cannot produce such a state of feeling, that to abstain from groaning is impossible? The answer was: "Yes, but He never does." Then the Apostle Paul was egregiously deceived when he wrote about "groanings which cannot be uttered." Edwards was deceived when he wrote his book upon revivals. Revivals are all in the dark. Now, no man who reviews the history of the Church will adopt such a sentiment. I do not like this attempt to shut out, or stifle, or keep down, or limit, the spirit of prayer. I would sooner cut off my right hand than rebuke the spirit of prayer, as I have heard of its being done by saying: "Do not let me hear any more groaning!"

# CHAPTER V

## PREVAILING PRAYER

*" The effectual fervent prayer of a righteous man availeth much."*
—James. v. 16.

1. THERE are two kinds of means requisite to promote a revival: the one to influence men, the other to influence God. The truth is employed to influence men, and prayer to move God. When I speak of moving God, I do not mean that God's mind is changed by prayer, or that His disposition or character is changed. But prayer produces such a change in us as renders it consistent for God to do as it would not be consistent for Him to do otherwise. When a sinner repents, that state of feeling makes it proper for God to forgive him. God has always been ready to forgive him on that condition, so that when the sinner changes his feelings and repents, it requires no change of feeling in God to pardon him. It is the sinner's repentance that renders His forgiveness proper, and is the occasion of God's acting as he does.

2. Others err in the reverse direction. Not that they lay too much stress on prayer. But they overlook the fact that prayer might be offered for ever, by itself, and nothing would be done.

Many people go away into their rooms alone "to pray," simply because "they must say their prayers." The time has come when they are in the habit of going by themselves for prayer—in the morning, or at noon, or at whatever time of day it may be. But instead of having anything to say, any definite object before their mind, they fall down on their knees and pray for just what comes into their minds

37

—for everything that floats in the imagination at the time, and when they have done, they can hardly tell a word of what they have been praying for. This is not effectual prayer.

3. To pray effectually you must pray with submission to the will of God. Do not confound submission with indifference. No two things are more unlike. I once knew an individual who came where there was a revival. He himself was cold, and did not enter into the spirit of it, and had no spirit of prayer; and when he heard the brethren pray as if they could not be denied, he was shocked at their boldness, and kept all the time insisting on the importance of praying with submission; when it was as plain as anything could be that he confounded submission with indifference.

4. While the will of God is not known, to submit, without prayer, is tempting God. Perhaps, and for aught you know, the fact of your offering the right kind of prayer may be the thing on which the event turns. In the case of an impenitent friend, the very condition on which he is to be saved from hell may be the fervency and importunity of your prayer for that individual.

5. Prevailing prayer is often offered in the present day, when Christians have been wrought up to such a pitch of importunity and such a holy boldness that when they look back upon it afterwards, they were frightened and amazed at themselves, to think they should have dared to exercise such importunity with God. And yet these prayers have prevailed, and obtained the blessing. And many of these persons, with whom I am acquainted, are among the holiest persons I know in the world.

6. The temptation to selfish motives is so strong that there is reason to fear a great many parental prayers never rise above the yearnings of parental tenderness. And that

is the reason why so many prayers are not answered and why so many pious, praying parents have ungodly children. Much of the prayer for the heathen world seems to be based on no higher principle than sympathy. Missionary agents and others are dwelling almost exclusively upon the millions of heathens going to hell, while little is said of their dishonouring God.

7. Most Christians come up to prevailing prayer by a protracted process. Their minds gradually become filled with anxiety about an object, so that they will even go about their business sighing out their desires to God. Just as the mother whose child is sick goes round her house sighing as if her heart would break. And if she is a praying mother, her sighs are breathed out to God all the day long. If she goes out of the room where her child is, her mind is still on it; and if she is asleep, still her thoughts are on it, and she starts in her dreams, thinking that perhaps it may be dying. Her whole mind is absorbed in that sick child. This is the state of mind in which Christians offer prevailing prayer.

8. The spirit of those that have been in distress for the souls of others, so far as I can discern, seems not to be different from that of the apostle, who travailed for souls, and was ready to wish himself accursed from Christ for others. (Rom. ix. 3). Nor from that of the Psalmist (Psa. cxix. 53): "Horror hath taken hold upon me, because of the wicked that forsake Thy law." And (ver. 136): "Rivers of waters run down mine eyes, because they keep not Thy law." Nor from that of the prophet Jeremiah (iv. 19): "My bowels, my bowels! I am pained at my very heart; my heart maketh a noise in me: I cannot hold my peace, because Thou hast heard, O my soul, the sound of the trumpet, the alarm of war." And so in chapters ix. 1, and xiii. 17; and Isa. xxii. 4. We read of Mordecai, when he saw his people

in danger of being destroyed with a temporal destruction (Esth. iv. 1), that he "rent his clothes, and put on sackcloth with ashes, and went out into the midst of the city, and cried with a loud and a bitter cry." And why then should persons be thought to be distracted when they cannot forbear crying out at the consideration of the misery of those that are going to eternal destruction?

(*Note.*—This would fitly apply to John Livingstone ("Livingstone of Shotts"), who spent the whole night prior to June 21, 1630, in prayer and conference, being designated to preach next day at the Kirk of Shotts. When alone in the fields, about eight o'clock in the morning, he began to steal away, in an agony of fear, when the overcoming power of the Spirit constrained him to return. He accordingly preached, as arranged; his text being Ezekiel xxxvi. 25, 26. After he had been speaking for an hour and a half a few drops of rain disconcerted the people, but Livingstone, asking the people if they had any shelter from the storm of God's wrath, went on for another hour. There were about five hundred converted on the spot. It is an illustration of revival being linked to revival that at the great meeting at Kilsyth (of which place Livingstone was a native), on July 23, 1839, William Chalmers Burns, preaching on Psalm cx. 3, retold the story of the Kirk of Shotts, and pressed immediate acceptance of Christ. "I felt my own soul moved in a manner so remarkable," said Burns, "that I was led, like Mr. Livingstone, to plead with the unconverted instantly to close with God's offer of mercy. . . . The power of the Lord's spirit became so mighty upon their souls as to carry all before it, like the 'rushing mighty wind' of Pentecost. Some were screaming out in agony; others—and among these strong men—fell to the ground as if they had been dead. I was obliged to give out a psalm, our voices being mingled with the mourning groans of many prisoners sighing for deliverance.")

9. If you mean to pray effectually, you must pray a great deal. It was said of the Apostle James that after he was dead it was found that his knees were callous, like a camel's knees, by praying so much. Ah, here was the secret of the success of those primitive ministers! They had callous knees!

10. If you intend prayer to be effectual, you must offer it in the name of Christ. You cannot come to God in your

own name. You cannot plead your own merits. But you can come in a Name that is always acceptable. You all know what it is to use the name of a man. If you should go to the bank with a draft or note, endorsed by a millionaire, that would be giving you his name, and you know you could get the money from the bank just as well as he could himself. Now, Jesus Christ gives you the use of His name. And when you pray in the name of Christ the meaning of it is, that you can prevail just as well as He could Himself, and receive just as much as God's well-beloved Son would if He were to pray Himself for the same things. But you must pray in faith.

11. These strong desires that I have described are the natural results of great benevolence and clear views regarding danger of sinners. It is perfectly reasonable that it should be so. If the women who are present should look up yonder and see a family burning to death in a fire, and hear their shrieks, and behold their agony, they would feel distressed, and it is very likely that many would faint away with agony. And nobody would wonder at it, or say they were fools, or crazy people, to feel so much distressed at such an awful sight. It would be thought strange if there were not some expressions of powerful feeling. Why is it any wonder, then, if Christians should feel as I have described when they have clear views of the state of sinners, and the awful danger they are in? The fact is, that those individuals who never have felt so, have never felt much real benevolence, and their piety must be of a very superficial character. I do not mean to judge harshly, or to speak unkindly, but I state it as a simple matter of fact; and people may talk about it as they please, but I know such piety is superficial. This is not censoriousness, but plain truth.

12. When Christians are driven to extremity, they make a desperate effort, roll the burden upon the Lord Jesus Christ,

and exercise a child-like confidence in Him. Then they feel
relieved; then they feel as if the soul they were praying for
would be saved. The burden is gone, and God seems in
kindness to soothe the mind with a sweet assurance that the
blessing will be granted. Often, after a Christian has had
this struggle, this agony in prayer, and has obtained relief
in this way, you will find the sweetest and most heavenly
affections flow out—the soul rests sweetly and gloriously in
God, and "rejoices with joy unspeakable and full of glory"
(1 Pet. i. 8).

(*Note.*—Chatham Street Theatre, New York, a haunt of blasphemy
and vice, was purchased by a committee, which included the brothers
Arthur and Lewis Tappan, and other friends of Finney's. It was
during the height of the great revival of 1831 (said Dr. T. L. Cuyler)
that two gentlemen called on the lessee and proposed to buy the place.
"What do you want it for?" said he. "For a Church," they replied.
"A w-h-a-t?" he inquired, aghast. "A Church," they reiterated.
The astonished man broke into tears and exclaimed: "You may have
it, and I will give you a thousand dollars towards it." At the close of
a morning rehearsal, the beautiful hymn, "The Voice of Free Grace,"
was sung, and Mr. Tappan announced to the actors that there would
be preaching that night upon that stage. When the house was
dedicated to the service of God, Finney preached on: "Who is on
the Lord's side?" The bar-room was changed into a prayer-room,
and the first convert was an actor. For some years the building was
used for services, Finney continuing to preach there until the erection
of the Broadway Tabernacle.)

13. This travailing in birth for souls creates also a remarkable bond of union between warm-hearted Christians and
the young converts. Those who are converted appear very
dear to the hearts that have had this spirit of prayer for
them. The feeling is like that of a mother for her first-born.
Paul expresses it beautifully when he says: "My little
children, of whom I travail in birth again"—they had back-
slidden, and he has all the agonies of a parent over a wander-
ing child—"I travail in birth again until Christ be formed
in you." In a revival, I have often noticed how those who

had the spirit of prayer loved the young converts. I know this is all so much algebra to those who have never felt it.

14. Another reason why God requires this sort of prayer is, that it is the only way in which the Church can be properly prepared to receive great blessings without being injured by them. When the Church is thus prostrated in the dust before God, and is in the depth of agony in prayer, the blessing does them good. While at the same time, if they had received the blessing without this deep prostration of soul, it would have puffed them up with pride. But as it is, it increases their holiness, their love, their humility.

15. Take a fact which was related in my hearing by a minister. He said that in a certain town there had been no revival for many years; the Church was nearly extinct, the youth were all unconverted, and desolation reigned unbroken. There lived, in a retired part of the town, an aged man, a blacksmith by trade, and of so stammering a tongue that it was painful to hear him speak. On one Friday, as he was at work in his shop, alone, his mind became greatly exercised about the state of the Church and of the impenitent. His agony became so great that he was induced to lay by his work, lock the shop door, and spend the afternoon in prayer.

He prevailed, and on the Sabbath called on the minister and desired him to appoint a "conference meeting." After some hesitation, the minister consented; observing, however, that he feared but few would attend. He appointed it the same evening at a large private house. When evening came, more assembled than could be accommodated in the house. All were silent for a time, until one sinner broke out in tears, and said, if any one could pray, would he pray for him? Another followed, and another, and still another, until it was found that persons from every quarter of the town were under deep conviction. And what was remarkable was, that they all dated their conviction at the hour that the old man was praying in his shop. A powerful revival followed. Thus this old stammering man prevailed, and as a prince had power with God.

# CHAPTER VI

### THE PRAYER OF FAITH

*" Therefore I say unto you, What things soever ye desire when ye pray, believe that ye receive them, and ye shall have them."*
—Mark xi. 24.

1. THERE are general promises and principles laid down in the Bible which Christians might make use of, if they would only think. Whenever you are in circumstances to which the promises or principles apply, there you are to use them. A parent finds this promise: "The mercy of the Lord is from everlasting to everlasting upon them that fear Him, and His righteousness unto children's children; to such as keep His covenant, and to those that remember His commandments to do them" (Ps. ciii. 17, 18). Now, here is a promise made to those who possess a certain character. If any parent is conscious that this is his character, he has a rightful ground to apply it to himself and his family. If you have this character, you are bound to make use of this promise in prayer, and believe it, even to your children's children.

2. Where there is any prophetic declaration that the thing prayed for is agreeable to the will of God; when it is plain from prophecy that the event is certainly to come, you are bound to believe it, and to make it the ground for your special faith in prayer. If the time is not specified in the Bible, and there is no evidence from other sources, you are not bound to believe that it shall take place now, or immediately. But if the time is specified, or if the time may be learned from the study of the prophecies, and it appears to have arrived, then Christians are under obligation to understand and apply it, by offering the prayer of faith.

For instance, take the case of Daniel, in regard to the return of the Jews from captivity. What does he say? "I Daniel understood by books the number of the years, whereof the word of the Lord came to Jeremiah the prophet, that He would accomplish seventy years in the desolations of Jerusalem" (Dan. ix. 2). Here he learned from books; that is, he studied his Bible, and in that way understood that the length of the captivity was to be seventy years.

3. What does he do then? Does he sit down upon the promise, and say: "God has pledged Himself to put an end to the captivity in seventy years, and the time has expired, and there is no need of doing anything"? Oh, no. He says: "And I set my face unto the Lord God, to seek by prayer and supplications, with fasting, and sackcloth, and ashes" (verse 3). He set himself at once to pray that the thing might be accomplished. He prayed in faith. But what was he to believe? What he had learned from the prophecy. There are many prophecies yet unfulfilled, in the Bible, which Christians are bound to understand, as far as they are capable of understanding them, and then make them the basis of believing prayer. Do not think, as some seem to do, that because a thing is foretold in prophecy it is not necessary to pray for it, or that it will come whether Christians pray for it or not. God says, in regard to this very class of events, which are revealed in prophecy: "I will yet for this be inquired of by the house of Israel, to do it for them" (Ezek. xxxvi. 37).

4. *When the Spirit of God is upon you*, and excites strong desires for any blessing, you are bound to pray for it *in faith*. You are bound to infer, from the fact that you find yourself drawn to desire such a thing while in the exercise of such holy affections as the Spirit of God produces, that these desires are the work of the Spirit. People are not apt to desire with the right kind of desires, unless they are excited

by the Spirit of God. The apostle refers to these desires, excited by the Spirit, in his Epistle to the Romans, where he says: "Likewise the Spirit also helpeth our infirmities: for we know not what we should pray for as we ought: but the Spirit itself maketh intercession for us with groanings which cannot be uttered" (Rom. viii. 26).

5. It is evident that the prayer of faith will obtain the blessing, from the fact that our faith rests on evidence that to grant that thing is the will of God. Not evidence that something else will be granted, but that this particular thing will be. But how, then, can we have evidence that this thing will be granted, if another thing is to be granted? People often receive more than they pray for. Solomon prayed for wisdom, and God granted him riches and honour in addition. So, a wife sometimes prays for the conversion of her husband, and if she offers the prayer in faith, God may not only grant that blessing, but convert her child, and her whole family. Blessings seem sometimes to "hang together," so that if a Christian gains one he gets them all.

I could name many individuals who have set themselves to examine the Bible on this subject, who, before they got half through with it, have been filled with the spirit of prayer. They found that God meant by His promises just what a plain, common-sense man would understand them to mean. I advise you to try it. You have Bibles; look them over, and whenever you find a promise that you can use, fasten it in your mind before you go on; and you will not get through the Book without finding out that God's promises mean just what they say.

6. *You must persevere.* You are not to pray for a thing once and then cease, and call that the prayer of faith. Look at Daniel. He prayed twenty-one days, and did not cease till he had obtained the blessing. He set his heart and his face unto the Lord, to seek by prayer and supplications,

with fasting, and sackcloth, and ashes; and he held on three weeks, and then the answer came. And why did not it come before? God sent an Archangel to bear the message, but the devil hindered him (Dan. x. 11–14). See what Christ says in the Parable of the Unjust Judge, and the Parable of the Loaves. What did He teach us by them? Why, that God will grant answers to prayer when it is importunate. "Shall not God avenge His own elect, which cry day and night unto Him?" (Luke xviii. 7).

Said a good man (Father Nash) to me: "Oh, I am dying for the want of strength to pray! My body is crushed, the world is on me, and how can I forbear praying?" I have known that man go to bed absolutely sick, for weakness and faintness, under the pressure. And I have known him pray as if he would do violence to heaven, and then have seen the blessing come as plainly in answer to his prayer as if it were revealed, so that no person would doubt it any more than if God had spoken from heaven. Shall I tell you how he died? He prayed more and more; he used to take the map of the world before him, and pray, and look over the different countries and pray for them, till he absolutely expired in his room, praying. Blessed man! He was the reproach of the ungodly, and of carnal, unbelieving professors; but he was the favourite of heaven, and a prevailing prince in prayer.

7. But you ask: "For whom are we to pray this prayer? We want to know in what cases, for what persons, and places, and at what times, we are to make the prayer of faith." I answer, as I have already answered: "When you have evidence—from promises, or prophecies, or providences, or the leadings of the Spirit—that God will do the things for which you pray."

8. "Did you not say there was a promise which pious parents may apply to their children? Why is it, then,

that so many pious parents have had impenitent children, who died in their sins?" Granted that it is so, what does it prove? "Let God be true, but every man a liar." (Rom. iii. 4). Which shall we believe, that God's promise has failed, or that these parents did not do their duty? Perhaps they did not believe the promise, or did not believe there was any such thing as the prayer of faith. Wherever you find a professor who does not believe in any such prayer, you find, as a general thing, that he has children and domestics yet in their sins.

9. "Will not these views lead to fanaticism? Will not many people think they are offering the prayer of faith when they are not?" That is the same objection that Unitarians make against the doctrine of regeneration— that many people think they have been born again when they have not. It is an argument against all spiritual religion whatever. Some think they have it when they have not, and are fanatics. But there are those who know what the prayer of faith is, just as there are those who know what spiritual experience is, though it may stumble cold-hearted professors who know it not. Even ministers often lay themselves open to the rebuke which Christ gave to Nicodemus: "Art thou a master in Israel, and knowest not these things?" (John iii. 10).

10. Persons who have not known by experience what the prayer of faith is, have great reason to doubt their own piety. This is by no means uncharitable. Let them examine themselves. It is to be feared that they understand prayer as little as Nicodemus did the New Birth. They have not walked with God, and you cannot describe it to them, any more than you can describe a beautiful painting to a blind man.

11. There is reason to believe that millions are in hell because professors have not offered the prayer of faith.

When professors had promises under their eyes, they have not had faith enough to use them. The signs of the times, and the indications of Providence, were favourable, perhaps, and the Spirit of God prompted desires for the salvation of souls. There was evidence enough that God was ready to grant a blessing, and if professors had only prayed in faith, God would have granted it; but He turned it away, because they would not discern the signs of the times.

12. I knew a father who was a good man, but had erroneous views respecting the prayer of faith; and his whole family of children were grown up, without one of them being converted. At length his son sickened, and seemed about to die. The father prayed, but the son grew worse, and seemed sinking into the grave without hope. The father prayed, till his anguish was unutterable. He went at last and prayed (there seemed no prospect of his son surviving) so that he poured out his soul as if he would not be denied, till at length he got an assurance that his son would not only live, but be converted; and that not only this one, but his whole family would be converted to God. He came into the house, and told his family his son would not die. They were astonished at him. "I tell you," said he, "he will not die. And no child of mine will ever die in his sins." That man's children were all converted, years ago.

What do you think of that? Was that fanaticism? If you believe so, it is because you know nothing about the matter. Do you pray so? Do you live in such a manner that you can offer such prayers for your children? I know that the children of professors may sometimes be converted in answer to the prayers of somebody else. But ought you to live so? Dare you trust to the prayers of others, when God calls you to sustain this important relation to your children?

13. Finally: see what combined effort is made to dispose of the Bible. The wicked are for throwing away the threatenings of the Bible, and the Church the promises. And what is there left? Between them, they leave the Bible a blank. I ask it in love: "What is our Bible good for, if we do not lay hold of its precious promises, and use them as the ground of our faith when we pray for the blessing of God?" You had better send your Bibles to the heathen, where they will do some good, if you are not going to believe and use them.

# CHAPTER VII

*"And whatsoever ye shall ask in My name, that will I do, that the Father may be glorified in the Son. If ye shall ask anything in My name, I will do it."*—John xiv. 13, 14.

1. GOD has so constituted us, and such is the economy of His grace, that we are sympathetic beings, and communicate our feelings to one another. A minister, for instance, will often, as it were, breathe his own feelings into his congregation. The Spirit of God that inspires his soul, makes use of his feelings to influence his hearers, just as much as He makes use of the words he preaches. So He makes use of the feelings of Christians. Nothing is more calculated to beget a spirit of prayer than to unite in social prayer with one who has the Spirit himself; unless this one should be so far ahead that his prayer will repel the rest. His prayer will awaken them, if they are not so far behind as to revolt at it and resist it. If they are anywhere near the standard of his feelings, his spirit will kindle, and burn, and spread all around. One individual who obtains the spirit of prayer will often arouse a whole Church, and extend the same spirit through the whole, so that a general revival follows.

2. Give up the meeting to the Spirit of God. Those who desire to pray, let them pray. If the leader sees anything that needs to be set right, let him remark, freely and kindly, and put it right, and then go on again. Only he should be careful to time his remarks, so as not to interrupt the flow of feeling, or to chill the meeting, or to turn the thoughts of the people from the proper subject.

3. Commonly, those who pray long in a meeting do so, not because they have the spirit of prayer, but because they have not. Some men will spin out a long prayer in telling God who and what He is, or they pray out a whole system of divinity. Some preach; others exhort the people— till everybody wishes they would stop, and God wishes so, too, most undoubtedly. They should keep to the point, and pray for what they came to pray for, and not follow the imagination of their own hearts all over the universe.

## Things Which May Defeat the Prayer-Meeting

4. *When there is an unhappy want of confidence in the leader*, there is no hope of any good. Whatever may be the cause, whether he is to blame or not, the very fact that he leads the meeting will cast a damp over it and prevent all good. I have witnessed it in Churches, where there was some offensive elder or deacon (perhaps justly deemed offensive; perhaps not) set to lead, and the meeting would die under his influence. If there is a want of confidence in regard to his piety, or in his ability, or in his judgment, or in anything connected with the meeting, everything he says or does will fall to the ground. The same thing often takes place where the Church has lost confidence in the minister.

5. *Persons coming late to the meeting.* This is a very great hindrance. When people have begun to pray, and their attention is fixed, and they have shut their eyes and closed their ears, to keep out everything from their minds, in the midst of a prayer somebody will come bolting in and walk through the room. Some will look up, and all have their minds interrupted for the moment. Then they all get fixed again, and another comes in, and so on. I suppose the devil would not care how many Christians

went to a prayer-meeting, if they would only go after the
meeting had begun. He would be glad to have ever so
many go "scattering along" in such a way, dodging in
very piously and distractingly.

6. *A great deal of singing often injures a prayer-meeting.*
The agonising spirit of prayer does not lead people to
sing. There is a time for everything; a time to sing, and
a time to pray. But if I know what it is to travail in birth
for souls, Christians never feel less like singing than when
they have the spirit of prayer for sinners.

7. Often a prayer-meeting is injured by *calling on the
young converts to sing joyful hymns.* This is highly improper
in a prayer-meeting. It is no time for them to let feeling
flow away in joyful singing; while so many sinners around
them, and their own former companions, are going down
to hell. A revival is often put down by the Church and
the minister giving themselves up to singing with young
converts. Thus, by stopping to rejoice when they ought to
feel more and more deeply for sinners, they grieve away
the Spirit of God, and they soon find that their agony and
travail of soul are gone.

8. *Prayer-meetings are often too long.* They should
always be dismissed while Christians have feeling, and not
be spun out until all feeling is exhausted, and the spirit of
prayer is gone.

Every minister ought to know that if the prayer-meetings
are neglected, all his labours are in vain. Unless he can
get Christians to attend the prayer-meetings, all else that
he can do will not improve the state of religion.

9. *Prayer-meetings are the most difficult meetings* to sustain
—as, indeed, they ought to be. They are so spiritual that
unless the leader be peculiarly prepared, both in heart
and mind, they will dwindle. It is in vain for the leader
to complain that members of the Church do not attend.

In nine cases out of ten it is the leader's fault that they do not attend. If he felt as he ought they would find the meeting so interesting that they would attend as a matter of course. If he is so cold, and dull, and lacking in spirituality, as to freeze everything, no wonder people do not come to the meeting. Church officers often complain and scold because people do not come to the prayer-meeting, when the truth is, they themselves are so cold that they freeze to death everybody who does come.

10. *The great object of all the means of grace is to aim directly at the conversion of sinners.* You should pray that they may be converted *there*. Do not pray that they may be merely awakened and convicted, but that they may be converted *on the spot*. No one should either pray, or make any remarks, as if he expected a single sinner would go away without giving his heart to God. You should all make the impression on his mind, that *now* he must submit. If you do this while you are yet speaking God will hear.

# CHAPTER VIII

## HINDRANCES TO REVIVALS

*"And I sent messengers unto them, saying, I am doing a great work, so that I cannot come down : why should the work cease, whilst I leave it, and come down to you ?"*—Nehemiah vi. 3.

1. *When Christians get proud of their "great revival," it will cease.* I mean those Christians who have been instrumental in promoting it. It is almost always the case in a revival, that a part of the Church proves too proud or too worldly to take any part in the work. They are determined to stand aloof, and wait, and see what it will come to. The pride of this part of the Church cannot stop the revival, for the revival never rested on them. It began without them, and it can go on without them. They may fold their arms and do nothing but look out and find fault; and still the work may go on.

But when the part of the Church that does the work begins to think what a great revival they have had, how they have laboured and prayed, how bold and how zealous they have been, and how much good they have done, then the work will be likely to decline. Perhaps it has been published in the papers what a revival there has been in that Church, and how absorbed the members have been, so they think how high they will stand in the estimation of other Churches, all over the land, because they have had such a great revival. And so they get puffed up, and vain, and they can no longer enjoy the presence of God. The Spirit withdraws from them, and the revival ceases.

2. *When Christians begin to proselytise.* Perhaps a revival will go on for a time, and all sectarian difficulties are

banished, till somebody circulates a book, privately, to gain proselytes. Perhaps some over-zealous deacon, or some mischief-making woman, or some proselytising minister, cannot keep still any longer, but begins to work the work of the devil, by attempting to gain proselytes, and so stirs up bitterness; and, raising a selfish strife, grieves away the Spirit, and drives Christians into parties. No more revival there!

3. *The Spirit may be grieved by a spirit of boasting of the revival.* Sometimes, as soon as a revival commences, you will see it blazed out in the newspapers. And most commonly this will kill the revival. There was a case in a neighbouring State, where a revival commenced, and instantly there came out a letter from the pastor, telling that he had a revival. I saw the letter, and said to myself: "That is the last we shall hear of this revival." And so it was. In a few days the work totally ceased. I could mention cases and places, where persons have published such things as to puff up the Church, and make the people so proud that little more could be done for the revival.

4. *Some, under pretence of publishing things to the praise and glory of God*, have published things that savoured so strongly of a disposition to exalt themselves—making their own agency stand out conspicuously—as were evidently calculated to make an unhappy impression. At a protracted meeting held in this Church, a year ago last fall, there were five hundred hopefully converted, whose names and places of residence we knew. A considerable number of them joined this Church. Many of them united with other Churches. Nothing was said of this in the papers. I have several times been asked why we were so silent on the subject. I could only reply, that there was such a tendency to self-exaltation in the Churches that I was afraid to publish anything on the subject. Perhaps I erred. But I have so

often seen mischief done by premature publications, that I thought it best to say nothing about it.

5. *A revival may be expected to cease, when Christians lose the spirit of brotherly love.* Jesus Christ will not continue with people in a revival any longer than they continue in the exercise of brotherly love. When Christians are in the spirit of a revival, they feel this love, and then you will hear them call each other "Brother" and "Sister," very affectionately. But when they begin to get cold, they lose this warmth and glow of affection for one another, and then this calling "Brother" and "Sister" will seem silly, and they will leave it off. In some Churches they never call each other so; but where there is a revival Christians naturally do it. I never saw a revival, and probably there never was one, in which they did not do it. But as soon as this begins to cease, the Spirit of God is grieved, and departs from among them.

6. *Christians of all denominations should lay aside prejudice.* Vast multitudes of professors of religion have indulged prejudice to such a degree as to be unwilling to read and hear, and come to a right understanding on the subject. But Christians cannot pray in this state of mind. I defy any one to possess the spirit of prayer while he is too prejudiced to examine this or any other question of duty. If the light did not shine, Christians might remain in the dark upon this point, and still possess the spirit of prayer. But if they refuse to come to the light, they cannot pray. Where ministers, individual Christians, or whole Churches, resist truth upon this point, when it is so extensively diffused and before the public mind, I do not believe they will or can enjoy a revival of religion.

7. Ordinarily, a protracted meeting should be conducted throughout by the *same minister* if possible. Sometimes through courtesy, visiting ministers are asked to speak, and there has been no blessing. The reason has been obvious.

They did not come in a state of mind which was right for entering into such work; and they did not know the state of people's minds, so as to know what to preach. Suppose a person who is sick should call a different physician every day. Neither would know what the symptoms had been, what was the course of the disease or of the treatment, what remedies had been tried, or what the patient could bear. The method would certainly kill the patient. Just so in a protracted meeting, carried on by a succession of ministers. None of them get into the spirit of it, and generally they do more harm than good.

A protracted meeting should not, ordinarily, be appointed, unless they can secure the right kind of help, and get a minister or two who will agree to stay on the ground till the meeting is finished. Then they will probably secure a rich blessing.

(*Note.*—The "anxious seat" was a sore subject of contention among the alleged "new measures." A striking instance of this opposition was seen at Rochester, N.Y. A judge, of much influence in the place, especially among its many lawyers, warmly opposed the method of invitation, yet he attended the meetings regularly, and Finney cherished the hope that he would be converted. One night the judge vacated his seat, and Finney, who was preaching a sermon specially applicable to him, concluded that he had gone home. Presently, however, Finney felt his coat pulled, and he found, just behind him, the judge, who said: "Mr. Finney, please pray for me by name; also, I will go to the anxious seat." The effect was electrical as the judge made his way to the front of the pulpit and knelt down. Prayer and weeping prevailed through the meeting, and the judge was immediately joined by many—lawyers and others—who crowded to the front, filling every place where there was room to kneel. Finney was naturally interested in the conversion of lawyers, and expressed the opinion that "in proportion to their numbers more of them have been converted than of any other class.")

Just so with the awakened sinner. Preach to him, and at the moment he thinks he is willing to do anything; he thinks he is determined to serve the Lord; but bring him to the test; call on him to do one thing, to take one step, that shall identify him with the people of God or cross his pride, and his pride comes up, and he refuses; his delusion is brought out, and he finds himself a lost sinner still; whereas, if you had not done it, he might have gone away flattering himself that he was a Christian. If you say to him: "There is the anxious seat, come out and avow your determination to be on the Lord's side," and if he is not willing to *do so small a thing as that, then he is not willing to do anything*, and there he is, brought out before his own conscience. It uncovers the delusion of the human heart, and prevents a great many spurious conversions, by showing those who might otherwise imagine themselves willing to do anything for Christ that in fact they are willing to do *nothing*.

The Church has always felt it necessary to have something of the kind to answer this very purpose. In the days of the apostles *baptism* answered this purpose. The Gospel was preached to the people, and then all those who were willing to be on the side of Christ were called on to be *baptised. It held the precise place that the anxious seat does now, as a public manifestation of a determination to be a Christian.*

In modern times, even those who have been violently to the *anxious seat* have been obliged to adopt *some substitute*, or they could not get along in promoting a revival. Some have adopted the expedient of inviting the people who were anxious for their souls, to *stay*, for conversation, after the rest of the congregation have retired. But what is the difference? This is as much setting up a test as the other. Others, who would be much ashamed to employ the anxious seat, have asked those who have any feeling on the subject to retain their seats when the rest retire. Others have called the anxious to withdraw into a lecture-room. The object of all these is the same, and the principle is the same—to bring people out from the refuge of false shame.

8. It is evident we must have more arousing preaching, to meet the character and wants of the age. Ministers are generally beginning to find this out. And some of them complain of it, and suppose it to be "owing to new measures," as they call them. They say that such ministers as our fathers would have been glad to hear, cannot now be heard, can neither obtain a pastorate nor secure an audience. And they think that new measures have perverted the taste of the people. But this is not the difficulty. The character of the age is changed, but these men retain the same *prosy style* of preaching that answered half a century ago.

Look at the early Methodists. Many of their ministers are unlearned, in the common sense of the term—many of them taken right from the shop or farm, and yet they have gathered congregations, and pushed their way, and won souls everywhere. Wherever the Methodists have gone, their plain, pointed and simple, but warm and animated mode of preaching has always gathered congregations. Few Presbyterian ministers have gathered such large assemblies, or won so many souls. Now, are we to be told that we must pursue the same old, formal mode of doing things, amidst all these changes? As well might the north river be rolled back, as the world converted under such preaching. Those who adopt a different style of preaching, as the Methodists have done, will run away from us. We must have powerful preaching, or the devil will have the people, except what the Methodists can save! Many ministers are finding out already that a Methodist preacher, without the advantages of a liberal education, will draw a congregation around him which a Presbyterian minister, with perhaps ten times as much learning, cannot equal, because he has not the earnest manner of the other, and does not pour out fire upon his hearers when he preaches. (Would to God that the Methodists were the same to-day.—E. E. S.)

9. *Other things which may stop a Revival.* Some have talked very foolishly on this subject, as if nothing could hinder a genuine revival. They say: "If your revival is a work of God, it cannot be stopped: can any created being stop God?" Now I ask if this is common sense? Formerly, it used to be the established belief that a revival could not be stopped, because it was the work of God. And so they supposed it would go on, whatever might be done to hinder it, in the Church or out of it. But the farmer might just as well reason so, and think he could go and cut down his wheat and not hurt the crop, because it is God that makes grain grow. A revival is the work of God, and so is a crop of wheat; and God is as much dependent on the use of means in one case as the other. And therefore a revival is as liable to be injured as a wheat field. A revival will cease whenever *Christians become mechanical in their attempts to promote it.* When their faith is strong, and their hearts are warm and mellow, and their prayers full of holy emotion, and their words with power, then the work goes on. But when their prayers begin to be cold and without emotion, and they begin to labour mechanically, and to use words without feeling, then the revival will cease.

10. The revival will stop when the Church *gets exhausted by labour.* Multitudes of Christians commit a great mistake here in time of revival. They are so thoughtless, and have so little judgment, that they will break up all their habits of living, neglect to eat and sleep at the proper hours, and let the excitement run away with them, so that they overdo their bodies, and are so imprudent that they soon become exhausted, and it is impossible for them to continue in the work. Revivals often cease from negligence and imprudence, in this respect, on the part of those engaged in carrying them on, and declensions follow.

11. When Christians *do not feel their dependence on the*

*Spirit.* Whenever they get strong in their own strength, God curses their blessings. In many instances, they sin against their own mercies because they get lifted up with their success, and take the credit to themselves, and do not give all the glory to God. As He says: "If ye will not hear, and if ye will not lay it to heart, to give glory unto My name, saith the Lord of hosts, I will even send a curse upon you, and I will curse your blessings; yea, I have cursed them already, because ye do not lay it to heart" (Mal. ii. 2). There has been a great deal of this, undoubtedly. I have seen many thing in the papers that suggested a disposition in men to take credit for success in promoting revivals. There is doubtless a great temptation to this, and it requires the utmost watchfulness, on the part of ministers and Churches, to guard against it, and not to grieve the Spirit away by vainglorying in men.

12. A revival will decline and cease, unless Christians are frequently revived. By this I mean, that Christians, in order to keep in the spirit of revival, commonly need to be frequently convicted and humbled and broken down before God. This is something which many do not understand, when we talk about a Christian being revived. But the fact is, that in a revival, the Christian's heart is liable to get crusted over, and lose its exquisite relish for divine things; his unction and prevalence in prayer abate, and then he must be renewed over again. It is impossible to keep him in such a state as not to do injury to the work, unless he passes through such a process every few days. I have never laboured in revivals in company with any one who would keep in the work and be fit to manage a revival continually, who did not pass through this process of breaking down as often as once in two or three weeks.

13. Revivals can be put down *by the continued opposition of the Old School, combined with a bad spirit in the New*

*School*. If those who do nothing to promote revivals continue their opposition, and if those who are labouring to promote them allow themselves to get impatient, and get into a bad spirit, the revival will cease. When the Old School write letters in the papers against revivals or revival men, and the New School write letters back again in a contentious spirit, revivals will cease. LET THEM KEEP ABOUT THEIR WORK, and neither talk about the opposition, nor preach upon it, nor rush into print about it. If others choose to publish "slang," let the Lord's people keep to their work. None of the slander will stop the revival, while those who are engaged in it mind their business, and keep to the work.

14. Show me a minister that has taken ground against the Temperance reformation who has had a revival. Show me one who now stands aloof from it who has a revival. Show me one who now temporises upon this point, who does not come out and take a stand in favour of Temperance, who has a revival. It used not to be so. But now the subject has come up, and has been discussed, and is understood, no man can shut his eyes upon the truth. The man's hands are RED WITH BLOOD who stands aloof from the Temperance cause. And can *he* have a revival?

15. Another thing that hinders revivals is, *neglecting the claims of Missions*. If Christians confine their attention to their own Church, do not read even their missionary magazine or use any other means to inform themselves on the subject of the claims of the world, but reject the light, and will not do what God calls them to do in this cause, the Spirit of God will depart from them.

16. If the Church wishes to promote revivals, *she must sanctify the Sabbath*. There is a vast deal of Sabbath-breaking in the land. Merchants break it, travellers break it, the Government breaks it. A few years ago an attempt

was made in the western part of this State to establish and sustain a Sabbath-keeping line of boats and coaches. But it was found that the *Church* would not sustain the enterprise. Many professors of religion would not travel in these coaches, and would not have their goods forwarded in canal-boats that would be detained from travelling on the Sabbath. At one time, Christians were much engaged in petitioning Congress to suspend the Sabbath mails, and now they seem to be ashamed of it. But one thing is most certain, that unless something is done, and done speedily, and done effectually, to promote the sanctification of the Sabbath by the Church, the Sabbath will go by the board, and we shall not only have our mails running on the Sabbath, and post-offices open, but, by and by, our courts of justice, and halls of legislation, will be kept open on the Sabbath. And what can the Church do, what will this nation do, *without any Sabbath?*

# CHAPTER IX

## TO WIN SOULS REQUIRES WISDOM

*He that winneth souls is wise.*—Proverbs xi. 30.

DEALING with Careless Sinners.

1. In regard to the *time*. It is important that you should select a proper time to try to make a serious impression on the mind of a careless sinner. For if you fail of selecting the most proper time, very probably you will be defeated.

2. It is desirable, if possible, to address a person who is careless, *when he is disengaged from other employments.*

3. It is important to take a person, if possible, at a time when he *is not strongly excited with any other subject*. Otherwise he will be in an unfit frame to be addressed on the subject of religion.

4. Be sure that the person is *perfectly sober*. It used to be more common than it is now for people to drink spirits every day, and become more or less intoxicated. Precisely in proportion as they are so, they are rendered unfit to be approached on the subject of religion. If they have been drinking beer, or cider, or wine, so that you can smell their breath, you may know there is little chance of producing any lasting effect on them, for when thus affected they are very fond of talking upon religion.

5. If possible, where you wish to converse with a man on the subject of salvation, take him when he *is in a good temper*. If you find him out of humour, very probably he will get angry and abuse you. Better let him alone for that time.

6. If possible, always take an opportunity to converse with careless sinners when they are *alone*. Most men are too proud to be conversed with freely respecting themselves in the presence of others, even their own family.

7. In visiting families, instead of calling all the family together at the same time to be talked to, the better way is to see them all, *one at a time*.

There was a pious woman who kept a boarding-house for young gentlemen; she had twenty-one or two of them in her house, and at length she became very anxious for their salvation. She made it a subject of prayer, but saw no seriousness among them. At length she saw that there must be something done besides praying, and yet she did not know what to do. One morning, after breakfast, as the rest were retiring, she asked one of them to stop a few minutes. She took him aside, and conversed with him tenderly on the subject of religion, and prayed with him. She followed up the impression made, and pretty soon he was hopefully converted. Then she spoke to another, and so on, taking one at a time, and letting none of the rest know what was going on, so as not to alarm them, till all these young men were converted to God. Now, if she had brought the subject before the whole of them together, very likely they would have turned it all into ridicule; or perhaps they would have been offended and left the house, and then she could have had no further influence over them. But taking one alone, and treating him respectfully and kindly, he had no such motive for resistance as arises out of the presence of others.

8. *Be solemn!* Avoid all lightness of manner or language. Levity will produce anything but a right impression. You ought to feel that you are engaged in a very solemn work, which is going to affect the character of your friend or neighbour, and probably determine his destiny for eternity.

Who could trifle and use levity in such circumstances, if his heart were sincere?

9. *Be respectful.* Some seem to suppose it necessary to be abrupt, and rude, and coarse, in their intercourse with the careless and impenitent. No mistake can be greater. The apostle Peter had given us a better rule on the subject, where he says: "Be pitiful, be courteous: not rendering evil for evil, or railing for railing: but contrariwise blessing" (I Pet. iii 8, 9).

10. Bring the great and *fundamental truths* to bear upon the person's mind. Sinners are very apt to run off upon some pretext, or some subordinate point, especially one of sectarianism.

Tell him the present business is to save his soul, and not to settle controversial questions in theology. Hold him to the great fundamental points, by which he must be saved or lost.

11. Bring up the individual's *particular sins*. Talking in general terms against sin will produce no results. You must make a man feel that you mean *him*. A minister who cannot make his hearers feel that he means them, cannot expect to accomplish much. Some people are very careful to avoid mentioning the particular sins of which they know the individual to be guilty, for fear of hurting his feelings. This is wrong. If you know his history, bring up his particular sins; kindly but plainly; not to give offence, but to awaken conscience, and give full force to the truth.

12. It is generally *best to be short*, and not spin out what we have to say. Get the attention as soon as you can to the very point; say a few things and press them home, and bring the matter to an issue. If possible, get them to repent and give themselves to Christ at the time. This is the proper issue. Carefully avoid making an impression that you do not wish them to repent *now*.

13. Wherever you have reason to believe that a person within your reach is awakened, do not sleep till you have poured in the light upon his mind, and have tried to bring him to *immediate repentance*. Then is the time to press the subject with effect.

14. Sometimes there is some *particular sin* which he will not forsake. He pretends it is only a small one; or tries to persuade himself it is no sin at all. No matter how small it is, he can never get into the kingdom of God till he gives it up. Sometimes an individual has seen it to be a sin to use tobacco, and he can never find true peace till he gives it up. Perhaps he is looking upon it as a small sin. But God knows nothing about small sins in such a case. What is the sin? It is injuring your health, and setting a bad example; and you are taking God's money (which you are bound to employ in His service) and spending it for tobacco. What would a merchant say if he found one of his clerks in the habit of going to the money drawer, and taking money enough to keep him in cigars? Would he call it a small offence? No; he would say the clerk deserved to be sent to the State prison. I mention this particular sin, because I have found it to be one of the things to which men who are convicted will hold on, although they know it to be wrong, and then wonder why they do not find peace.

15. So, individuals are sometimes entrenched in a determination that they will not go to a *particular meeting* (perhaps the inquiry meeting, or some prayer-meeting); or they will not have a certain person to pray with them; or they will not take a particular seat, such as the "anxious seat." They say they can be converted just as well without yielding this point, for religion does not consist in going to a particular meeting, or taking a particular attitude in prayer, or a particular seat. This is true; but by taking this ground they make it the material point. And so long as they are

entrenched there, and determined to bring God to their terms, they never can be converted. Sinners will often yield anything else, and do anything else, and do anything in the world but yield the point upon which they have taken a stand against God. They cannot be humbled, until they yield this point, whatever it is. And if, without yielding, they get a hope, it will be a false hope.

16. Sometimes persons will strenuously maintain that they have committed *the unpardonable sin*. When they get that idea into their minds, they will turn everything you say against themselves. In some such cases, it is a good way to take them on their own ground, and reason with them in this way: "Suppose you have committed the unpardonable sin, what then? It is reasonable that you should submit to God, and be sorry for your sins, and break off from them, and do all the good you can, even if God will not forgive you. Even if you go to hell, you ought to do this." Press this thought until you find they understand and consent to it.

It is common for persons in such cases to keep their eyes on *themselves;* they will shut *themselves up*, and keep looking at their own darkness, instead of looking away to Christ. Now, if you can take their minds off from themselves, and get them to think of Christ, you may draw them away from brooding over their own present feelings, and get them to lay hold on the hope set before them in the Gospel.

17. The Church is now filled up with hypocrites, because people were never made to see that unless they made an *entire consecration* of all to Christ—all their time, all their talents, all their influence—they would never get to heaven. Many think they can be Christians, and yet dream along through life, and use all their time and property for themselves, only giving a little now and then, just to save appear-

ances, and when they can do it with perfect convenience. But it is a sad mistake, and they will find it so, if they do not employ their energies for God. And when they die, instead of finding heaven at the end of the path they are pursuing, they will find hell there.

18. Here is a point where almost all ministers fail. They know not how to wake up the Church, and raise the tone of piety to a high standard, and thus clear the way for the work of conversion. Many ministers can preach to sinners very well, but gain little success, for the counter-acting influence of the Church resists it all, and they have not skill enough to remove the difficulty. There is only *here and there a minister in the country who knows how to probe the Church when it is in a cold, backslidden state,* so as to effectually awaken the members and keep them awake.

The members of the Church sin against such light, that when they become cold it is very difficult to rouse them up. They have a form of piety which wards off the truth, while at the same time it is just that kind of piety which has no power or efficiency. Such professors are the most difficult individuals to arouse from their slumbers. I do not mean that they are always more wicked than the impenitent. They are often employed about the machinery of religion, and pass for very good Christians, but they are of no use in a revival.

19. To reach different classes of sinners successfully requires great wisdom on the part of a minister. For instance, a sermon on a particular subject may impress a particular class of persons among his hearers. Perhaps they will begin to look serious, or to talk about it, or to cavil about it. Now, if the minister is wise, he will know how to observe those indications, and to follow right on, with sermons adapted to this class, until he leads them into the

kingdom of God. Then, let him go back and take another class, find out where they are hid, break down their refuges, and follow them up, till he leads them, also, into the kingdom. He should thus beat about every bush where sinners hide themselves, as the voice of God followed Adam in the garden: "ADAM, WHERE ART THOU?" till one class of hearers after another is brought in, and so the whole community is converted.

Now, a minister must be very wise to do this.

*Those are the best educated ministers, who win the most souls.* Ministers are sometimes looked down upon, and called very ignorant, because they do not know sciences and languages; although they are very far from being ignorant of the great thing for which the ministry is appointed. This is wrong! Learning is important, and always useful. But after all, a minister may know how to win souls to Christ without great learning; and he has the best education for a minister who can win the most souls to Christ.

20. *When young men come out of the seminaries, are they fit to go into a revival?* Look at a place where there has been a revival in progress, and a minister is wanted. Let them send to a theological seminary for a minister. Will he enter into the work, and sustain it, and carry it on? Seldom! Like David with Saul's armour, he comes in with such a load of theological trumpery that he knows not what to do. Leave him there for two weeks, and the revival is at an end. The Churches know and feel that the greater part of these young men do not know how to do anything that needs to be done for a revival, and the complaint is made that the young ministers are so far behind the Church. You may send all over the United States, to theological seminaries, and find but few young ministers fitted to carry forward the work. What a state of things!

21. And here I would say, that to my own mind it appears evident, that unless our *theological professors preach a good deal*, mingle much with the Church, and sympathise with her in all her movements, it is morally, if not naturally, impossible, that they should succeed in training young men to the spirit of the age. It is a shame and a sin, that theological professors, who preach but seldom, who are withdrawn from the active duties of the ministry, should sit in their studies and write their letters, advisory or dictatorial, to ministers and Churches who are in the field and who are in circumstances to judge what needs to be done. The men who spend all, or at least a portion, of their time in the active duties of the ministry, are the only men who are able to judge of what is expedient or inexpedient, prudent or imprudent, as to measures, from time to time. It is as dangerous and ridiculous for our theological professors, who are withdrawn from the field of conflict, to be allowed to dictate, in regard to the measures and movements of the Church, as it would be for a general to sit in his bedchamber and attempt to order a battle.

22. Finally: I wish to ask, Who among you can lay any claim to the possession of this *divine wisdom?* Who among you, laymen? Who among you, ministers? Can any of you? Can I? Are we at work, wisely, to win souls? Or are we trying to make ourselves believe that success is no criterion of wisdom?

How few of you have ever had wisdom enough to convert so much as a single sinner? Do not say: "I cannot convert sinners. God alone can convert sinners." Look at the text: "He that winneth souls is wise." It is true that God converts sinners. But there is a sense, too, in which ministers convert them.

Men! Women! You are bound to be wise in winning souls. Perhaps already souls have perished, because you have not put forth the wisdom which you might in saving them. The city is going to hell. Yes, the world is going to hell, and must go on, till the Church finds out what to do to win souls.

# CHAPTER X

### HOW TO APPROACH SINNERS

*"Behold, I send you forth as sheep in the midst of wolves : be ye therefore wise as serpents, and harmless as doves."*—Matthew x. 16.

SEIZE the *earliest opportunity* to converse with those around you who are careless. Do not put it off from day to day, thinking a better opportunity will come. You must *seek* an opportunity, and if none offers, make one. Appoint a time or place, and get an interview with your friend or neighbour, where you can speak to him freely. Send him a note; go to him on purpose; make it look like a matter of business— as if you were in earnest in endeavouring to promote his soul's salvation. Then he will feel that it is a matter of importance, at least in your eyes. Follow it up till you succeed, or become convinced that, for the time, nothing more can be done.

When you approach a careless individual, be sure to treat him *kindly*. *Let him see* that you address him, not because you seek a quarrel with him, but because you love his soul and desire his best good in time and eternity. If you are harsh and overbearing in your manner, you will probably offend him, and drive him farther off from the way of life.

Be sure to be *very plain*. Do not suffer yourself to cover up any circumstance of the person's character, and his relations to God. Lay it all open, not for the purpose of offending or wounding him, but because it is necessary. Before you can cure a wound, you must probe it to the bottom. Keep back none of the truth, but let it come out plainly before him.

*Be very patient.* If he has a real difficulty in his mind, be very patient till you find out what it is, and then clear it up. If what he alleges is a mere cavil, make him see that it is a cavil. Do not try to answer it by argument, but show him that he is not sincere in advancing it. It is not worth while to spend your time in arguing against a cavil; make him feel that he is committing sin to plead it, and thus enlist his conscience on your side.

Be careful to *guard your own spirit.* There are many people who have not good temper enough to converse with those who are much opposed to religion. And such a person wants no better triumph than to see you angry. He will go away exulting because he has "made one of these saints mad."

If the sinner is inclined to entrench himself against God, be careful *not to take his part in anything.* If he says he cannot do his duty, do not take sides with him, or say anything to countenance his falsehood; do not tell him he cannot, or help to maintain himself in the controversy against his Maker. Sometimes a careless sinner will commence finding fault with Christians; do not take his part, do not side with him against Christians. Just tell him he has not their sins to answer for: he had better see to his own concerns. If you agree with him, he feels that he has you on his side. Show him that it is a wicked and censorious spirit that prompts him to make these remarks, and not a regard for the honour of the religion or the laws of Jesus Christ.

Sometimes the individual has some idol, something which he loves more than God, which prevents him from giving himself up. You must search out and see what it is that he will not give up. Perhaps it is *wealth;* perhaps some *earthly friend;* perhaps *gay dress* or *gay company*, or some *favourite amusement.* At any rate, there is something on which his heart is so set that he will not yield to God.

They may have *entrenched* themselves somewhere, and fortified their minds in regard to some particular point, which they are determined not to yield. For instance, they may have taken strong ground that they will not do a particular thing. I knew a man who was determined not to go into a certain grove to pray. Several other persons during the revival had gone into the grove, and there, by prayer and meditation, given themselves to God. His own clerk had been converted there. The lawyer himself was awakened, but he was determined that he would not go into that grove. He had powerful convictions, and went on for weeks in this way, with no relief. He tried to make God believe that it was not pride that kept him from Christ; and so, when he was going home from meeting he would kneel down in the street and pray. And not only that, but he would look round for a mud-puddle in the street, in which he might kneel, to show that he was not proud. He once prayed *all night* in his parlour—but he would not go into the grove. His distress was so great, and he was so wroth with God, that he was strongly tempted to make away with himself, and actually threw away his knife for fear he should cut his throat. At length he concluded he would go into the grove and pray; and as soon as he got there he was converted, and poured out his full heart to God.

(*Note.*—This was Mr. Benjamin Wright, in whose office Finney studied law, "his own clerk" being, of course, Finney himself. "I have a parlour to pray in," said the lawyer; "I am not going into the woods." However, he gave in; and a young man who happened to overhear him in the wood came to Finney, in the village, crying: "Squire Wright is converted! I heard some one shouting very loudly, and I saw Squire Wright pacing to and fro and singing as loudly as he could sing; and every few moments he would stop and clap his hands with his full strength and shout: 'I will rejoice in the God of my salvation!'" Presently the lawyer came into his office, crying: "I've got it! I've got it!" From that time he took a decided stand for God.)

Make it an object of *constant study, and of daily reflection, and pray* to learn how to deal with sinners so as to promote their conversion. It is the great business on earth of every Christian to save souls. People often complain that they do not know how to take hold of this matter. Why, the reason is plain enough; they have never studied it. They have never taken the proper pains to qualify themselves for the work. If people made it no more a matter of attention and thought to qualify themselves for their worldly business, than they do to save souls, how do you think they would succeed? *Now, if you are thus neglecting the* MAIN BUSINESS *of life, what are you living for ?* If you do not make it a matter of study, how you may most successfully act in building up the kingdom of Christ, you are acting a very wicked and absurd part as a Christian.

Anxious sinners are to be regarded as being in a very *solemn and critical state.* They have, in fact, come to a turning-point. It is a time when their destiny is likely to be settled for ever. Christians ought to feel deeply for them. *In many respects their circumstances are more solemn than those of the Judgment. Here their destiny is settled. The Judgment Day reveals it.* And the particular time when it is done is when the *Spirit is striving with them.*

# CHAPTER XI

## THE NECESSITY OF UNION

*" Again I say unto you, That if two of you shall agree on earth as touching anything that they shall ask, it shall be done for them of My Father which is in heaven."*—Matthew xviii. 19.

1. An individual may desire a revival, for the glory of God and the salvation of sinners. Another member of the Church may also desire a revival, but from very different motives. Some, perhaps, desire a revival in order to have the congregation built up and strengthened, so as to make it more easy for them to pay their expenses in supporting the Gospel. Another desires a revival for the sake of having the Church increased so as to be more numerous and more respectable. Others desire a revival because they have been opposed or evil spoken of, and they wish to have it known that whatever may be thought or said, God blesses them. Sometimes people desire a revival from mere natural affection, so as to have their friends converted and saved.

2. Sometimes they are engaged in prayer for a revival, and you would think by their earnestness and union that they would certainly move God to grant the blessing, till you find out their reason. And what is it? Why, they see their congregation is about to be broken up, unless something can be done. Or they see some other denomination gaining ground, and there is no way to counteract this but by having a revival in their Church. All their praying is therefore only an attempt to get the Almighty to help them out of their difficulty; it is purely selfish and therefore offensive to God.

3. Parents never agree in praying for the conversion of their children in such a way as to have their prayers answered,

until they feel that their children are rebels. Parents often pray very earnestly for their children, because they wish God to save them, and they almost think hardly of God if He does not save their children. But if they would have their prayers prevail, they must come to take God's part against their children, even though for their perverseness and incorrigible wickedness He should be obliged to send them to hell. I knew a woman who was very anxious for the salvation of her son, and she used to pray for him with agony, but still he remained impenitent, until at length she became convinced that her prayers and agonies had been nothing but the fond yearnings of parental feeling, and were not dictated at all by a just view of her son's character as a wilful and wicked rebel against God. And there was never any impression made on his mind until she was made to take strong ground against him as a rebel, and to look on him as deserving to be sent to hell. And then he was converted. The reason was, she never before was influenced by the right motive.

4. Suppose a Church gets the idea that sinners are poor, unfortunate creatures, who come into the world with such a nature that they cannot help sinning, and that sinners are just as unable to repent and believe the Gospel as they are to fly to the moon, how can it be felt that the sinner is a rebel against God, and that he deserves to be sent to hell? How can they feel that the sinner is to blame? And how can they take God's part when they pray? If they do not take God's part against the sinner, they cannot expect God will regard their prayers, for they do not pray with right motives. No doubt one great reason why so many prayers are not answered, is, that those who pray do in fact take the sinner's part against God. They pray as if the sinner were a poor, unfortunate being, to be pitied, rather than as if he were a guilty wretch, to be blamed.

And the reason is, that they do not believe sinners are able to obey God.

5. How often do you hear people pray for sinners in this style: "O Lord, help this poor soul to do what he is required to do; O Lord, enable him to do so-and-so." Now this language implies that they take the sinner's part, and not God's. They cannot pray successfully, until they understand that the sinner is a rebel, and obstinate in his rebellion—so obstinate, that he never will, without the Holy Spirit, do what he might, as well as not, instantly do, and that this obstinacy is the reason, and the only reason, why he needs the influence of the Holy Spirit for his conversion. The only ground on which the sinner needs divine agency is, to overcome his obstinacy, and make him willing to do what he can do, and what God justly requires him to do.

6. If there are rotten members in the Church, they should be removed, and the Church should agree to cut them off. If they remain, they are such a reproach to religion as to hinder a revival. Sometimes when an attempt is made to cast them out, this creates a division, and thus the work is stopped. Sometimes the offenders are persons of influence, or they have family friends who will take their part, and make a party, and thus create a bad spirit, and prevent a revival.

7. *In mutual confessions.* Whenever wrong has been done to any, there should be a full confession. I do not mean a cold and forced acknowledgment, such as saying: "If I have done wrong, I am sorry for it"; but a hearty confession, going the full length of the wrong, and showing that it comes out of a broken heart.

8. *Forgiveness of enemies.* A great obstruction to revivals is often found in the fact that active and leading individuals harbour a revengeful and unforgiving spirit towards those who have injured them.

But let the members of the Church be truly agreed, in confessing their faults, and in cherishing a tender, merciful, forgiving, Christlike spirit towards any who, they think, have done them wrong, and then the Spirit will come down upon them not by measure.

(*Note.*—In all Finney's writings we find him urgent and expectant on the subject of immediate conversion. In his address the effect appears to have been still more intense. For instance, Dr. Joseph T. Thompson (one of Finney's successors at Broadway Tabernacle) said of him: "He was unconsciously dramatic, never theatrical. One of the most impressive sermons I ever heard him deliver was on the text: 'Judgment also will I lay to the line, and righteousness to the plummet: and the hail shall sweep away the refuge of lies' (Isa. xxviii. 17). Right before our eyes, he conjured up such a storm of wind, rain, and hail that I grew chilled through and through. I shivered and buttoned up my coat. . . . I was never more astonished than when I went outside and saw the world bathed in sunlight, the birds twittering, and all as calm and serene as a June day could ever be. How he did it I cannot tell." Again, Dr. Cuyler said: "Finney's sermons were chain lightning, flashing conviction into the hearts of the stoutest sceptics, and the links of his logic were so compact that they defied resistance.")

## CHAPTER XII

### DIRECTIONS TO SINNERS

*"What must I do to be saved?"*—Acts xvi. 30.

1. No direction should be given that does not include a change of heart, or a right heart, or hearty obedience to Christ. In other words, nothing is proper which does not imply actually becoming a Christian. Any other direction that falls short of this, is of no use. It will not bring him any nearer to the kingdom, it will do no good, but will lead him to deter the very thing which he must do in order to be saved. The sinner should be told plainly, at once, what he must do if he would not be lost; and he should be told nothing that does not include a right state of heart. Whatever you may do, sinner, that does not include a right heart, is sin. Whether you read the Bible or not, you are in sin, so long as you remain in rebellion. Whether you go to religious services or stay away; whether you pray or not, it is nothing but rebellion, every moment. It is surprising that a sinner should suppose himself to be doing service to God when he prays, and reads his Bible.

Should a rebel against the Government read the statute-book while he continues in rebellion, and has no design to obey; should he ask for pardon while he holds on to his weapons of resistance and warfare; would you think him doing his country a service, and lay it under obligation to show him favour? No; you would say that all his reading and praying were only an insult to the majesty both of the lawgiver and the law. So you, sinner, while you remain in impenitence, are insulting God, and setting him at defiance, whether you read His word, and pray, or let it alone. No matter what place or what attitude your body is in, on your knees or in the house of God; so long as your heart is not right, so long as you resist the Holy Ghost, and reject Christ, you are a rebel against your Maker.

2. It is generally in point, and a safe and suitable direction, to tell a sinner to repent. I say, generally. For sometimes the Spirit of God seems not so much to direct the sinner's attention to his own sins as to some other thing. In the days of the Apostles, the minds of the people seem to have been agitated mainly on the question, whether Jesus was the true Messiah. The Apostles therefore directed much of their instruction to this point, to prove that he was the Christ. Whenever anxious sinners asked them what they must do, they most commonly exhorted them to "believe on the Lord Jesus Christ." They bore down on this point, because here was where the Spirit of God was striving, and this was the subject that especially agitated the minds of the people, and, consequently, this would probably be the first thing a person would do on submitting to God. It was the grand point at issue between God and the Jew and Gentile of those days, whether Jesus Christ was the Son of God. It was the point in dispute. To bring the sinner to yield this controverted question was the way the most effectually to humble him.

3. At other times, it will be found that the Spirit of God is dealing with sinners chiefly in reference to their own sins. Sometimes He deals with them in regard to a particular duty, as prayer—perhaps family prayer. The sinner will be found to be contesting that point with God, whether it is right for him to pray, or whether he ought to pray in his family. I have known striking cases of this kind, where the individual was struggling on this point, and as soon as he fell on his knees to pray, he yielded his heart, showing

that this was the very point which the Spirit of God was contesting, and *the hinge* on which his controversy with God all turned. That was conversion.

4. Words that used to be plain, and easily understood, have now become so perverted that they need to be explained to sinners, or they will often convey a wrong impression to their minds. This is the case with the word "repentance." Many suppose that remorse, or a sense of guilt, is repentance. Then, hell is full of repentance, for it is full of remorse, unutterable and eternal. Others feel regret that they have done such a thing, and they call that repenting. But they only regret that they have sinned, because of the consequences, and not because they abhor sin. This is not repentance. Others suppose that conviction of sin and strong fears of hell are repentance. Others consider the remonstrances of conscience as repentance; they say: "I never do anything wrong without repenting and feeling sorry I did it."

Sinners must be shown that all these things are not repentance. They are not only consistent with the utmost wickedness, but the devil might have them all and yet remain a devil. Repentance is a change of mind, as regards God and towards sin. It is not only a change of views, but a change of the ultimate preference or choice of the soul. It is a voluntary change, and by consequence involves a change of feeling and of action toward God and toward sin. It is what is naturally understood by a change of mind on any subject of interest and importance. We hear that a man has changed his mind in politics; everybody understands that he has undergone a change in his views, his feelings, and his conduct. This is repentance, on that subject: it is a change of mind but not toward God. Evangelical repentance is a change of willing, of feeling, and of life, in respect to God.

5. Repentance always implies abhorrence of sin. It of course involves the love of God and the forsaking of sin. The sinner who truly repents does not feel as impenitent sinners think they would feel at giving up their sins, if they were to become religious. Impenitent sinners look upon religion in this way: that if they become pious, they should be obliged to stay away from balls and parties, and obliged to give up theatres, or gambling, or other things that they now take delight in. And they see not how they could ever enjoy themselves, if they should break off from all those things. But this is very far from being a correct view of the matter.

Religion does not make them unhappy, by shutting them out from things in which they delight, because the first step in it is to repent, to change their mind in regard to all these things. They do not seem to realise that the person who has repented has no disposition for these things; he has given them up, and turned his mind away from them. Sinners feel as if they should want to go to such places, and want to mingle in such scenes, just as much as they do now, and that it will be such a continual sacrifice as to make them unhappy. This is a great mistake.

6. I know there are some professors, who would be very glad to betake themselves to their former practices, were it not that they feel constrained, by fear of losing their character, or the like. But, mark me: if they feel so, it is because they have no religion; they do not hate sin. If they desire their former ways, they have no religion, they have never repented; for repentance always consists in a change of views and feelings. If they were really converted, instead of choosing such things, they would turn away from them with loathing. Instead of lusting after the flesh-pots of Egypt, and desiring to go into their former circles, parties, balls, and the like, they would find their highest pleasure in obeying God.

7. Another proper direction to be given to sinners, is to confess and forsake their sins. They must confess to God their sins against God, and confess to men their sins against men; and forsake them all. A man does not forsake his sins till he has made all the reparation in his power. If he has stolen money, or defrauded his neighbour out of property, he does not forsake his sins by merely resolving not to steal any more, or to cheat again; he must make reparation to the extent of his power. So, if he has slandered any one, he does not forsake his sin by merely saying he will not do so again; he must make reparation. So, in like manner, if he has robbed God, as all sinners have, he must make reparation, as far as he has power.

Suppose a man has made money in rebellion against God, and has withheld from Him his time, talents, and service, has lived and rioted upon the bounties of His providence, and refused to lay himself out for the salvation of the world; he has robbed God. Now, if he should die, feeling this money to be his own, and should he leave it to his heirs without consulting the will of God—why, he is just as certain to go to hell as a highway robber. He has never made any satisfaction to God. With all his whining and pious talk, he has never confessed HIS SIN to God, not forsaken his sin, for he has neither felt nor acknowledged himself to be the steward of God. If he refuses to hold the property in his possession as the steward of God; if he accounts it his own, and as such gives it to his children, he says in effect to God: "That property is not Thine, it is mine, and I will give it to my children." He has continued to persevere in his sin, for he does not relinquish the ownership of that of which he has robbed God.

What would a merchant think if his clerk should take all the capital and set up a store of his own, and die with it in his hands? Will such a man go to heaven? "No," you say. "God would prove Himself unjust, to let such a character go unpunished." What, then, shall we say of the man who has robbed God all his life? God sent him to be His clerk, to manage some of His affairs, but he has stolen all the money, and says it is his; he keeps it, and, dying, leaves it to his children, as if it were all his own lawful property. Has that man forsaken sin? I tell you, No! If he has not surrendered himself and all he has to God, he has not taken the first step in the way to heaven.

8. Sometimes sinners imagine they must wait for different feelings before they submit to God. They say: "I do not think I *feel* right yet to accept Christ." They ought to be made to see that what God requires of them is to *will* right. If they obey and submit with the will, the feelings will adjust themselves in due time. It is not a question of feeling, but of willing and acting.

The feelings are involuntary, and have no moral character except what they derive from the action of the will, with which action they sympathise. Before the will is right, the feelings will not be, of course. The sinner should come to Christ by accepting Him at once; and this he must do, not in obedience to his feelings, but in obedience to his conscience. Obey, submit, trust. Give up all instantly, and your feelings will come right. Do not wait for better feelings, but commit your whole being to God at once, and this will soon result in the feelings for which you are waiting. What God requires of you is the present act of your mind, in turning from sin to holiness, and from the service of Satan to the service of the living God.

# CHAPTER XIII

### FALSE COMFORTS FOR SINNERS

*"How then comfort ye me in vain, seeing in your answers there remaineth falsehood?"*—Job xxi. 34.

1. No doubt, millions and millions are now in hell, because there were those around them who gave them false comfort, who had so much false pity, or were themselves so much in the dark, that they would not let sinners remain in anxiety till they had submitted their hearts to God, but administered falsehood.

2. I have often had professors bring anxious sinners to me, and beg me to comfort them, and then, when I have probed the conscience of the sinner to the quick, they have shuddered, and sometimes taken his part. It is sometimes impossible to deal effectually with young people who are anxious, in the presence of their parents, because the parents have so much more compassion for their children than regard to the honour of God. This is a position which is all wrong; and with such views and feelings you had better hold your tongue than say anything to the anxious.

3. I have often met with cases of this kind. A mother will tell her son, who is anxious, what an obedient child he has always been, how good and how kind, and she begs him "not to take on so." So a husband will tell his wife, or a wife her husband: "How good you are!" and say: "Why, you are not so bad. You have been to hear that frightful minister, who frightens people, and you have got excited. Be comforted, for I am sure you have not been bad enough to justify such distress." When the truth is, they have been a great deal worse than they think they have.

No sinner ever has an idea of his sins greater than they really are. No sinner ever has an adequate idea of how great a sinner he is. It is not probable that any man could live under a full sight of his sins. God has, in mercy, spared all His creatures on earth that worst of sights, a naked human heart. The sinner's guilt is much more deep and damning than he thinks, and his danger is much greater than he thinks it is; and if he should see his sins as they are, probably he would not live one moment. True, a sinner may have false notions on the subject, which may create distress, but which have no foundation. He may think he has committed the unpardonable sin, or that he has grieved away the Spirit, or sinned away his day of grace. But to tell the most moral and naturally amiable person in the world that he is good enough, or that he is not so bad as he thinks he is, is not giving him rational comfort, but is deceiving him and ruining his soul.

4. The sinner is on the very verge of hell, he is in rebellion against God, and his danger is infinitely greater than he imagines. Oh, what a doctrine of devils it is to tell a rebel against heaven not to be distressed! What is all his distress but rebellion itself? He is not comforted, because he refuses to be comforted. God is ready to comfort him. You need not think to be more compassionate than God. He will fill the sinner with comfort, in an instant, on submission. There stands the sinner, struggling against God, and against the Holy Ghost, and against conscience, until he is distressed almost to death, but still he will not yield; and now some one comes in, saying: "Oh, I hate to see you feel so bad, do not be so distressed; cheer up, cheer up; religion does not consist in being gloomy; be comforted." Horrid!

5. People sometimes comfort a sinner by telling him: "If you are elected, you will be brought in." I once heard of a case where a person under great distress of mind was sent

to converse with a neighbouring minister. They talked for a long time. As the person went away, the minister said to him: "I should like to send a line by you to your father." His father was a pious man. The minister wrote the letter, and forgot to seal it. As the sinner was going home, he saw that the letter was not sealed, and he thought to himself, that probably the minister had written about him, and his curiosity at length led him to open and read it.

And there he found words to this purport: "Dear Sir,— I found your son under conviction, and in great distress, and it seems not easy to say anything to give him relief. But, if he is one of the elect, he is sure to be brought in." He had wanted to say something to comfort the father; but now, mark: that letter had wellnigh ruined the son's soul; for he settled down on the doctrine of Election, saying: "If I am elected, I shall be brought in"; and his conviction was gone. Years afterwards he was awakened and converted, but only after a great struggle, and never until that false impression had been obliterated from his mind, and he had been made to see that he had nothing at all to do with the doctrine of Election, but that if he did not repent he would be lost.

# CHAPTER XIV

## INSTRUCTIONS TO CONVERTS

*"Feed my lambs."*—John xxi. 15.

1. ONE of the first things young converts should be taught is to distinguish between emotion and principle in religion. I want you to get hold of the words, and have them fixed in your mind; to have you distinguish between emotion and principle.

2. By emotion, I mean that state of mind of which we are conscious, and which we call feeling—an involuntary state of mind, that arises, of course, when we are in certain circumstances or under certain influences. There may be high-wrought feelings, or they may subside into tranquillity, or disappear entirely. But these emotions should be carefully distinguished from religious principle. By principle, I do not mean any substance or root or seed or sprout implanted in the soul. But I mean the voluntary decision of the mind, the firm determination to fulfil duty and to obey the will of God, by which a Christian should always be governed.

3. When a man is fully determined to obey God, because it is RIGHT that he should obey God, I call that principle. Whether he feels any lively religious emotion at the time or not, he will do his duty cheerfully, readily, and heartily, whatever may be the state of his feelings. This is acting upon principle, and not from emotion. Many young converts hold mistaken views upon this subject, and depend almost entirely on the state of their feelings to go forward in duty. Some will not lead a prayer-meeting, unless they feel as if

they could make an eloquent prayer. Multitudes are influenced almost entirely by their emotions, and they give way to this, as if they thought themselves under no obligation to duty, unless urged on by some strong emotion. They will be very zealous in religion when they feel like it, when their emotions are warm and lively, but they will not act out religion consistently, and carry it into all the concerns of life. They are religious only as they are impelled by a gush of feeling. But this is not true religion.

4. Young converts should be carefully taught that when duty is before them they are to *do it*. However dull their feelings may be, if duty calls, Do It! Do not wait for feeling, but Do It!! Most likely the very emotions for which you would wait, will be called into exercise when you begin to do your duty. If the duty be prayer, for instance, and you have not the feelings you would wish, do not wait for emotions before you pray, but pray, and "open thy mouth wide" (Ps. lxxxi. 10); and in doing it, you are most likely to have the emotions for which you were inclined to wait, and which constitute the conscious happiness of religion.

5. Young converts should not be made sectarian in their feelings. They should not be taught to dwell upon sectarian distinctions, or to be sticklish about sectarian points. They ought to examine these points, according to their importance, at a proper time, and in a proper way, and make up their minds for themselves. But they should not be taught to dwell upon them, or to make much of them at the outset of their religious life.

When I hear them asking: "Do you believe in the doctrine of Election?" or: "Do you believe in sprinkling?" or: "Do you believe in immersing?" I feel sad. I never knew such converts to be worth much. Their sectarian zeal soon sours their feelings, eats out all the heart of their religion, and moulds their whole character into sinful, sectarian bigotry. They generally become mighty zealous for the traditions of the elders, and very little concerned for the salvation of souls.

6. Young converts should be taught that they have renounced the ownership of all their possessions, and of themselves, and that if they have not done this they are not Christians. They should not be left to think that anything is their own; their time, property, influence, faculties, body or soul. "Ye are not your own" (1 Cor. vi. 19); they belong to God; and when they submitted to God they made a free surrender of all to Him, to be ruled and disposed of at His pleasure. They have no right to spend one hour as if their time were their own; no right to go anywhere, or do anything, for themselves, but should hold all at the disposal of God, and employ all for the glory of God.

Until Christians, and the Churches generally, take the ground, and hold to it, that it is just as much a matter of discipline for a Church member practically to deny his stewardship as to deny the deity of Christ; and that covetousness, fairly proved, shall just as soon exclude a man from communion as adultery.

7. It is high time these matters were set right. And the only way to set them right is to begin with those who are just entering upon religion. Young converts must be told that they are just as worthy of condemnation (and that the Church can hold no fellowship with them), if they show a covetous spirit, and turn a deaf ear when the whole world is calling for help, as if they were living in adultery, or in the daily worship of idols.

8. They (young converts) should be taught to pray always, whatever may take place. For the want of right instruction on this point many young converts suffer loss and get far away from God. For instance, sometimes it happens that a

young convert will fall into some sin, and then he feels as if he could not pray, and instead of overcoming this he feels so distressed that he waits for the keen edge of his distress to pass away. Instead of going right to Jesus Christ in the midst of his agony, and confessing his sin out of the fulness of his heart, and getting a renewed pardon, and peace restored, he waits till all the keenness of his feelings has subsided; and then his repentance, if he does repent, is cold and half-hearted. Let me tell you, beloved, never to do this; but when your conscience presses you, go then to Christ, confess your sin fully, and pour out your heart to God.

Sometimes people will neglect to pray because they are in the dark, and feel no desire to pray. But that is the very time when they need prayer. That is the very reason why they ought to pray. You should go right to God and confess your coldness and darkness of mind. Tell Him just how you feel. Tell Him: "O Lord, I have no desire to pray, but I know I ought to pray." And immediately the Spirit may come and lead your heart out in prayer, and all the dark clouds will pass away.

9. Young converts should be faithfully warned against adopting a false standard in religion. They should not be left to fall in behind old professors, or keep such before their minds as a standard of holy living. They should always look at Christ as their model. Not aim at being as good Christians as the old Church members, and not think they are doing pretty well because they are as much awake as the old members of the Church; but they should aim at being holy. The Church has been greatly injured for the want of attention to this matter. Young converts have come forward, and their hearts were warm, and their zeal ardent enough to aim at a high standard, but they were not directed properly, and so they soon settled down into the notion

that what was good enough for others was good enough for them, and therefore they ceased to aim higher than those who were before them. And in this way the Church, instead of rising, with every revival, higher and higher in holiness, is kept nearly stationary.

10. Converts must learn to say "No." This is a very difficult lesson to many. See that young woman! Formerly she loved the gay circle, and took delight in its pleasures; she joined the Church, and then found herself aloof from all her old associates. They do not ask her now to their balls and parties, because they know she will not join them; and perhaps they keep entirely away for a time, for fear she should converse with them about their souls.

But, by and by, they grow a little bold, and some of them venture to ask her just to take a ride with a few friends. She does not like to say "No." They are her old friends, only a few of them are going, and surely a ride is so innocent a recreation that she may accept the invitation. But, now she has begun to comply, the ice is broken, and they have her again as one of them. It goes on, and she begins to attend their social visits—"only a few friends, you know" —till, by and by, the carpet is taken up for a dance; and the next thing, perhaps, she has gone for a sleigh ride on Saturday night, coming home after midnight, and then sleeping all the forenoon on the Sabbath to make up for it —perhaps Communion Sabbath, too. All for the want of learning to say "No."

11. See that young man! For a time he was always in his place in the Sabbath-school and in the prayer-meeting. But, by and by, his old friends begin to treat him with attention again, and they draw him along, step by step. He reasons that if he refuses to go with them in things that are innocent, he will lose his influence with them. And so he goes on,

till prayer-meeting, Bible-class, and even private Bible reading and prayer are neglected. Ah, young man, stop there! If you do not wish to expose the cause of Christ to scorn and contempt, learn to resist the *beginnings of temptation.*

12. It is of great importance that young converts should be taught to be strictly honest. It is being very different from the world at large, and different even from the great body of professors of religion. Alas, alas, how little conscience there is! How little of that real honesty, that pure, simple uprightness, which ought to mark the life of a child of God!

Look at this seriously. Who does God say will go to heaven? Read the fifteenth Psalm, and see. "He that sweareth to his own hurt, and changeth not." What do you think of that? If a man has promised anything, except it be to commit sin, let him keep his promise, if he means to be honest and to go to heaven. But these people will make promises, and because they cannot be prosecuted, will break them as if they were nothing. They would not let a cheque of theirs be returned from the bank. Why? Because they would lose credit, and would be sued.

Is this honest? Will such honesty as this get them admitted to heaven? What? Break your promises, and go up and carry a lie in your hand before God? If you refuse or neglect to fulfil your promise you are a liar; and if you persist in this, you shall have your part in the lake that burns with fire and brimstone. I would not for ten thousand worlds die with money in my hands that I had unrighteously withheld from any object to which I had promised it. Such money will "eat as doth a canker" (2 Tim. ii. 17).

If you are not able to pay the money, that is a good excuse. But then, say so. But if you refuse to pay what you have promised, because you have altered your mind, rely upon it, you are guilty. You cannot pray till you pay that money. Will you pray: "O Lord, I promised to give that money, but I altered my mind, and broke my promise; but still, O Lord, I pray Thee to bless me, although I keep my money, and make me happy in Thy love"? Will such prayers be heard? Never!

13. Religion does not consist in desires to do good actions. Desires that do not result in choice and action are not virtuous. Nor are such desires necessarily vicious. They may arise involuntarily in the mind, in view of certain objects; but while they produce no voluntary act, they are no more virtuous or vicious than the beating of the pulse, except in cases where we have indirectly willed them into existence, by voluntarily putting ourselves under circumstances calculated to excite them. The wickedest man on earth may have strong desires after holiness. Did you ever think of that? He may see clearly that holiness is the only and indispensable means of happiness. And the moment he apprehends holiness as a means of happiness, he naturally desires it. It is to be feared that multitudes are deceiving themselves with the supposition that a desire for holiness, as a means of happiness, is religion.

Many, doubtless, give themselves great credit for desires that never result in choosing right. They feel desires to do their duty, but do not choose to do it, because, upon the whole, they have still stronger desires not to do it. In such desires there is no virtue. An action or desire, to be virtuous in the sight of God, must be an act of the will. People often talk most absurdly on this subject, as though their desires had anything good, while they remain mere desires. "I think I desire to do so-and-so." But do you do it? "Oh, no, but I often feel a desire to do it." This is practical atheism.

14. Whatever desires a person may have, if they are not carried out into actual *choice and action*, they are not virtuous. And no degree of desire is itself virtuous. If this idea could be made prominent, and fully riveted in the minds of men, it would probably annihilate the hopes of half the members of the Churches, who are living on their good desires, while doing nothing for God.

15. Converts should be made to understand that *nothing which is selfish is religion*. Whatever desires they may have, and whatever choices and actions they may put forth, if, after all, the reason of them is selfish, there is no religion in them. A man may just as much commit sin in praying, or reading the Bible, or going to a religious service, as in anything else, if his motive is selfish. Suppose a man prays simply with a view to promote his own happiness. Is that religion? What is it but attempting to make God his Almighty Servant? It is nothing else but to attempt a great speculation, and to put the universe, God and all, under contribution to make him happy. It is the sublime degree of wickedness. It is so far from being piety that it is in fact superlative wickedness.

16. Nothing is acceptable to God, as religion, unless it is *performed heartily, to please God*. No outward action has anything good, or anything that God approves, unless it is performed from right motives and from the heart. Young converts should be taught fully and positively that all religion consists in obeying God from the heart. All religion consists in voluntary action. All that is holy, all that is lovely, in the sight of God, all that is properly called religion, consists in voluntary action, in voluntarily obeying the will of God from the heart.

17. Young converts should be taught that the *duty of self-denial* is one of the leading features of the Gospel. They should understand that they are not pious at all, any

further than they are willing to take up their cross daily, and deny themselves for Christ. There is but little self-denial in the Church, and the reason is that the duty is so much lost sight of, in giving instruction to young converts. How seldom are they told that self-denial is the leading feature in Christianity! In pleading for benevolent objects, how often will you find that ministers and agents do not even ask Christians to deny themselves for the sake of promoting the object! They only ask them to give what they can spare as well as not; in other words, to offer unto the Lord that which costs them nothing. What an abomination! They only ask for the surplus, for what is not wanted, for what can just as well be given as not.

18. Young converts should be taught so as to understand what Perseverance is. It is astonishing how people talk about perseverance. As if the doctrine of perseverance were: "Once in grace, always in grace"; or, "Once converted, sure to go to heaven." This is not the idea of Perseverance. The true idea is, that if a man is truly converted, he will, as a rule, CONTINUE to obey God; and, as a consequence, he will surely go to heaven. But if a person gets the idea that because he is "converted," therefore he will assuredly go to heaven, that man will almost assuredly go to hell.

Obedience to God consists in the state of the heart. It is being willing to obey God; willing that God should rule in all things. But if a man habitually disobeys God, in any one particular, he is in a state of mind that renders obedience in anything else impossible. To say that in some things a man obeys God, out of respect to His authority, and that in some other things he refuses obedience, is absurd.

19. Young converts are easily taught to be "temperate

in all things" (I Cor. ix. 25). Yet this is a subject greatly neglected in regard to young converts, and almost lost sight of in the Churches. Chewing and smoking tobacco are acts of intemperance. If they use these mere stimulants when there is no necessity for them, what is that but intemperance? That is not being "temperate in all things." Until Christians shall have a conscience on this subject, and be made to feel that they have no right to be intemperate in anything, they will make but little progress in religion. It is well known, or ought to be, that tea and coffee have no nutriment in them. They are mere stimulants. They go through the system without being digested. The milk and sugar you put in them are nourishing; and so they would be, just as much so, if you mixed them with rum, and made milk punch; but the tea and coffee afford no nourishment; and yet I dare say that a majority of the families in this city give more in a year for their tea and coffee than they do to save the world from hell.

Probably this is true respecting entire Churches. Even agents of benevolent societies will dare to go through the Churches soliciting funds, for the support of missionary and other institutions, and yet use tea, coffee, and, in some cases, tobacco. Strange! No doubt many are giving five times as much for mere intemperance as they give for every effort to save the world.

20. If professing Christians could be made to realise how much they spend for what are mere poisons, and nothing else, they would be amazed. Many persons will strenuously maintain that they cannot get along without these stimulants, these poisons, and they cannot give them up, no, not to redeem the world from eternal damnation. And very often they will absolutely show anger, if argued with, just as soon as the argument begins to pinch their consciences.

Oh, how long shall the Church show her hypocritical face at the missionary meeting, and pray God to save the world, while she is actually throwing away five times as much for sheer intemperance as she will give to save the world! Some of you may think these are little things, and that it is quite beneath the dignity of the pulpit to lecture against them. But I tell you it is a great mistake of yours if you think these are little things, when they make the Church odious in the sight of God, by exposing her hypocrisy and lust. Here is an individual who pretends he has given himself up to serve Jesus Christ, and yet he refuses to deny himself any darling lust, and then he will go and pray: "O Lord, save the world; O Lord, Thy Kingdom come!" I tell you it is hypocrisy. Shall such prayers be heard? Unless men are willing to deny themselves, I would not give a groat for the prayers of as many such professors as would cover the whole of the United States.

21. These things must be taught to young converts. It must come to this point in the Church, that men shall not be called Christians unless they will cut off the right hand, and pluck out the right eye, and deny themselves for Christ's sake. A little thing? See it poison the spirit of prayer! See it debase and sensualise the soul! Is that a trifle beneath the dignity of the pulpit, when these intemperate indulgences, of one kind and another, cost the Church five times, if not fifty times, more than all she gives for the salvation of the world?

An estimate has recently been made, showing that in the United States twenty millions of dollars' worth of coffee is consumed yearly; and who does not know that a great part of this is consumed by the Church. And yet grave ministers and members of Christian Churches are not ashamed to be seen countenancing this enormous waste of money; while at the same time the poor heathen are sending upon every wind of heaven their agonising wail for help. Heaven calls from above: "Go . . . preach the Gospel to every creature" (Mark xvi. 15). Hell groans from beneath, and ten thousand voices cry out from heaven, earth, and hell: "Do something to save the world!" Do it now! Oh, Now, or millions more are in hell through your neglect. And oh, tell it not in Gath, the Church, the ministry, will not deny even their lusts to save a world. Is this Christianity? What business have you to use Christ's money for such a purpose? Are you a steward? Who gave you this liberty? Look to it, lest it should be found at last that you have preferred self-gratification to obedience, and made a "god of your belly" (Phil. iii. 19).

22. The time to teach these things with effect is when the converts are young. If converts are not properly taught then, if they get a wrong habit, and begin with an easy, self-indulgent mode of living, it rarely happens that they become thoroughly reformed. I have conversed with old professors on these subjects, and have been astonished at their pertinacious obstinacy in indulging their lusts. And I am satisfied that the Church never can rise out of this sloth until young converts are faithfully taught, at the outset of their religious course, to be temperate in all things.

23. They should be taught that it is necessary for them to be just as holy as they think ministers ought to be. There has for a long time been an idea that ministers are bound to be holy and practise self-denial. And so they are. But it is strange they should suppose that ministers are bound to be any more holy than other people. They would be shocked to see a minister showing levity, or running after the fashions or getting out of temper.

They should aim at being perfect. Every young convert should be taught that if it is not his purpose to live without sin, he has not yet begun to be religious. What is religion but a supreme love to God and a supreme purpose of heart, or disposition to obey God? If there is not this, there is no religion at all. If any are prepared to say that they are perfect, all I have to say is: "Let them prove it." If they are so, I hope they will show it by their actions. (This perfection is not absolute perfection, but perfection in love. —E.E.S.)

24. But it is the duty of all to be perfect in motive, and to purpose entire, perpetual, and universal obedience to God. It should be their constant purpose to live wholly to God, and obey all His commandments. They should live so that if they should sin it would be an inconsistency, an exception, an individual case, in which they act contrary to the fixed and general purpose and tenor of their lives. They ought not to sin at all; they are bound to be as holy as God is if they expect to live with Him; and young converts should be taught to set out in the right course, or they will never be right.

(*Note.*—"A man may believe in what is really a state of entire sanctification," said Finney, "and aim at attaining it, although he may not call it by that name. Mrs. President Edwards, for example aimed at it, and manifestly attained it, and yet, such were her views of human infirmities, that she did not call her state one of entire sanctification. I care not what this state is called, if the thing be fully explained and insisted upon, together with the conditions of attaining it. Call it what you please: Christian perfection, heavenly-mindedness, the full assurance of faith or hope, or a state of entire consecration; by all these I understand the same thing.")

25. "You will not always feel as you do now." When the young convert is rejoicing in his Saviour, and calculating to live for the glory of God and the good of mankind, how often is he met with this reply: "You will not always feel so."

Thus, his mind is prepared to expect that he shall backslide, and not to be much surprised when he does. This is just the way the devil wants young converts dealt with, to have old Christians tell them: "Your feelings will not last, but, by and by, you will be as cold as we are." It has made my heart bleed to see it! When the young convert has been pouring out his warm heart to some old professor, and expecting the warm burstings of a kindred spirit responding to his own, what does he meet with? This cold answer, coming like a northern blast over his soul: "You will not always feel so." *SHAME! Just preparing the young convert to expect that he shall backslide as a matter of course: so that when he begins to decline, as under the very influences of this instruction it is most likely he will, it produces no surprise or alarm in his mind, but he looks at it just as a thing of course, doing as everybody else does.*

Such doctrine as this is the very last that should be taught to young converts. They should be told that they have only begun the Christian life, and that their religion is to consist in *going on in it.* They should be taught to go forward all the time, and "grow in grace" continually. Do not teach them to taper off their religion—to let it grow smaller and smaller till it comes to a point. *God says:* "The path of the just is as the shining light, that shineth more and more unto the perfect day" (Prov. iv. 18). Now whose path is that which grows dimmer and dimmer unto the perfect night? They should be brought to such a state of mind that the first indications of decay in spirituality or zeal will alarm them and spur them up to duty. There is no need that young converts should backslide as they do. Paul did not backslide. And I do not doubt that this very doctrine, "You will not always feel so," is one of the grand devices of Satan to bring about the result which it predicts.

26. *The very idea of being a Christian is to renounce self and*

*become entirely consecrated to God. A man has no more right to withhold anything from God than he has to rob or steal.* It is robbery in the highest sense of the term. It is an infinitely higher crime than it would be for a clerk in a store to go and take the money of his employer, and spend it on his own lusts and pleasures. *I mean, that for a man to withhold from God is a higher crime against HIM than a man can commit against his fellow-man, inasmuch as God is the Owner of all things in an infinitely higher sense than man can be the owner of anything.* If God calls on them to employ anything they have, their *money*, or their *time*, or to *give their children*, or to *dedicate themselves* in advancing His kingdom, and they refuse, because they want to use them in their own way, or prefer to do something else, it is vastly more blameable than for a clerk or an agent to go and embezzle the money that is entrusted him by his employer.

27. Young converts should be taught to *do all their duty*. They should never make a compromise with duty, nor think of saying: "I will do *this* as an offset for neglecting *that*." They should never rest satisfied till they have done their duties of every kind, in relation to their families, the Church, Sabbath Schools, the impenitent around them, the disposal of their property, and the conversion of the world. Let them do their duty, as they feel it when their hearts are warm; and never attempt to pick and choose among the commandments of God.

Teach them that religion does not consist *in raptures, or ecstasies*, or high flights of feeling. There may be a great deal of these where there *is* religion. But it ought to be understood that they are all involuntary emotions, and may exist in full power where there is *no* religion. They may be the mere workings of the imagination, without any truly religious affection at all. Persons may have them to such a degree as actually to swoon away with ecstasy, even on the subject of religion, without having any religion. I have known a person almost carried away with rapture, by a mere view of the natural attributes of God, His power and wisdom as displayed in the starry heavens, and yet the person had no religion. Religion is obedience to God, the voluntary submission of the soul to His will.

## CHAPTER XV

### BE FILLED WITH THE SPIRIT

"*Be filled with the Spirit*."—Ephesians v. 18.

### *Why Many Do Not Have the Spirit*

1. It may be that you live a hypocritical life. Your prayers are not earnest and sincere. Not only is your religion a mere outside show, without any heart, but you are insincere in your intercourse with others.

2. Others have so much levity that the Spirit will not dwell with them. The Spirit of God is solemn, and serious, and will not dwell with those who give way to thoughtless levity.

3. Others are so proud that they cannot have the Spirit. They are so fond of dress, high life, equipage, fashion, etc., that it is no wonder they are not filled with the Spirit.

4. Some are so worldly-minded, love property so well, and are trying so hard to get rich, that they cannot have the Spirit. How can He dwell with them when all their thoughts are on things of the world, and all their powers absorbed in procuring wealth? And when they get money they are pained if pressed by conscience to do something with it for the conversion of the world. They show how much they love the world in all their intercourse with others. Little things show it. They will screw down a poor man, who is doing a little piece of work for them, to the lowest penny, but if they are dealing on a large scale, very likely they will be liberal and fair, because it is for their advantage.

If it is a person they care not about—a labourer, or a mechanic, or a servant—they will grind him down to the last fraction, no matter what the work is really worth; and they actually pretend to make it a matter of conscience, that they cannot possibly give any more. Now, they would be ashamed to deal so with people of their own rank, because it would be known and injure their reputation; but God knows it, and has it all written down, that they are covetous and unfair in their dealings, and will not do right, only when it is for their interest. Now, how can such professors have the Spirit of God? It is impossible!

5. Others are neglecting some known duty, and that is the reason why they have not the Spirit. One does not pray in his family, though he knows he ought to do so, and yet he is trying to get the spirit of prayer!

If you have neglected any known duty, and thus lost the spirit of prayer, you must yield first. God has a controversy with you; you have refused obedience to God, and you must retract. You may have forgotten it, but God has not, and you must set yourself to recall it to mind and repent. God never will yield or grant you His Spirit till you repent. Had I an omniscient eye, I could call the names of the individuals in this congregation who have neglected some known duty (or committed some sin, that they have not repented of); and who are praying for the spirit of prayer, but cannot succeed in obtaining it.

6. If you know what it is by former experience to commune with God, and how sweet it is to dissolve in penitence and to be filled with the Spirit, you cannot but desire a return of those joys. And you may set yourself to pray earnestly for it, and to pray for a revival of religion. But, on the whole, you are unwilling it should come. You have so much to do that you cannot attend to it. Or it will require so many sacrifices that you cannot bear to have it. There are some

things you are not willing to give up. You find that if you wish to have the Spirit of God dwell with you, you must lead a different life; you must give up the world; you must make sacrifices; you must break off from your worldly associates, and make confession of your sins. And so, on the whole, you do not wish to have the Spirit come, unless He will consent to dwell with you and let you live as you please. But that He will never do.

7. Your guilt is just as great as the authority of God is great, which commands you: "Be filled with the Spirit." God commands it, and it is just as much a disobedience of God's commands as it would be to swear profanely, or steal, or commit adultery, or break the Sabbath. Think of that. And yet there are many people who do not blame themselves at all for not having the Spirit. They even think themselves quite pious Christians, because they go to prayer-meetings, and partake of the sacrament, and all that, though they live year after year without the Spirit of God. Now you see that the same God who says: "Do not get drunk," says also: "Be filled with the Spirit."

You all say, if a man is a habitual adulterer, or a thief, he is no Christian. Why? Because he lives in habitual disobedience to God. So, if he swears, you have no charity for him. You will not allow him to plead that his heart is right, and that words are nothing; that God does not care anything about words. You would think it outrageous to have such a man in the Church, or to have a company of such people pretend to call themselves a Christian Church. And yet they are not a whit more absolutely living in disobedience to God than you are, who live without the spirit of prayer and without the presence of God.

Your guilt is equal to all the good you might do if you were possessed by the Spirit of God in as great a measure as it is your duty to be, and as you might be. You are entirely responsible to the Church and to God for all this good that you might do. A man is responsible for all the good he *can* do.

8. You will be called eccentric; and probably you will deserve it. Probably you will really be eccentric. I never knew a person who was filled with the Spirit that was not called eccentric. And the reason is that such people are unlike other folk. There is therefore the best reasons why such persons should appear eccentric. They act under different influences, take different views, are moved by different motives, led by a different spirit. You are to expect such remarks. How often I have heard the remark respecting such-and-such persons: "He is a good man—but he is rather eccentric." I have sometimes asked for the particulars; in what does his eccentricity consist? I hear the catalogue, and it amounts to this, that he is spiritual. Make up your mind for this, to be "eccentric." There is such a thing as affected eccentricity. Horrible! But there is such a thing as being so deeply imbued with the Spirit of God that you must and will act so as to appear strange and eccentric to those who cannot understand the reasons of your conduct.

Paul was accused of being deranged by those who did not understand the views of things under which he acted. No doubt Festus thought the man was crazy, that "much learning had made him mad." But Paul said: "I am not mad, most noble Festus" (Acts xxvi. 24, 25). His conduct was so strange, so novel, that Festus thought it must be insanity. But the truth simply was, he saw the subject so clearly that he threw his whole soul into it. You must make up your mind to this, and so much the more as you live the more above the world and walk with God.

9. This is one of the most prominent and deeply-to-be-

deplored evils of the present day. The piety of the ministry, though real, is so superficial, in many instances, that the spiritual people of the Church feel that ministers do not, cannot, sympathise with them. The preaching does not meet their wants; it does not feed them. The ministers have not depth enough of religious experience to know how to search and wake up the Church; how to help those under temptation, to support the weak, to direct the strong.

When a minister has gone with a Church as far as his experience in spiritual exercises goes, there he stops; and until he has a renewed experience, his heart broken up afresh, and he set forward in the divine life and Christian experience, he will help them no more. He may preach sound doctrine, and so may an unconverted minister; but, after all, his preaching will want that searching pungency, that practical bearing, that unction which alone will reach the case of a spiritually-minded Christian. It is a fact over which the Church is groaning, that the piety of young men suffers so much in the course of their education, that when they enter the ministry, however much intellectual furniture they may possess, they are in a state of spiritual babyhood. They want nursing; they need rather to be fed, than to undertake to feed the Church of God.

10. If you have much of the Spirit of God, you must make up your mind to have much opposition, both in the Church and the world.

Very likely the leading men in the Church will oppose you. There has always been opposition in the Church. So it was when Christ was on earth. If you are far above their state of feeling, Church members will oppose you. If any man will live godly in Christ Jesus, he must expect persecution (2 Tim. iii. 12). Often the elders and even the minister will oppose you, if you are filled with the Spirit of God.

11. You must expect very frequent and agonising conflicts with Satan. Satan has very little trouble with those Christians who are not spiritual, but lukewarm, and slothful, and worldly-minded. And such do not understand what is said about spiritual conflicts. Perhaps they will smile when such things are mentioned. And so the devil lets them alone. They do not disturb him, nor he them. But spiritual Christians, he understands very well, are doing him a vast injury, and therefore he sets himself against them. Such Christians often have terrible conflicts. They have temptations that they never thought of before: blasphemous thoughts, atheism, suggestions to do deeds of wickedness, to destroy their own lives, and the like. And if you are spiritual, you may expect these terrible conflicts.

12. You will have greater conflicts with yourself than you ever thought of. You will sometimes find your own weaknesses making strange headway against the Spirit. "The flesh lusteth against the Spirit, and the Spirit against the flesh" (Gal. v. 17). Such a Christian (until sanctified wholly) is often thrown into consternation at the power of his own corruptions. One of the Commodores in the United States Navy was, as I have been told, a spiritual man; his pastor told me he had known that man lie on the floor and groan a great part of the night, in conflict with his own corruptions, and to cry to God, in agony, that He would break the power of the temptation. It seemed as if the devil was determined to ruin him, and his own heart, for the time being, was almost in league with the devil.

13. But, you will have peace with God. If the Church, and sinners, and the devil, oppose you, there will be One with whom you will have peace. Let you who are called

to these trials, and conflicts, and temptations, and who groan, and pray, and weep, and break your hearts, remember this consideration: your peace, so far as your feelings towards God are concerned, will flow like a river. You will likewise have peace of conscience, if you are led by the Spirit. You will not be constantly goaded and kept on the rack by a guilty conscience. Your conscience will be calm and quiet, unruffled as the summer's lake.

14. If filled with the Spirit, you will be useful. You cannot help being useful. Even if you were sick and unable to go out of your room, or to converse, and saw nobody, you would be ten times more useful than a hundred of those common sort of Christians who have no spirituality. A pious man in the western part of this State was suffering from consumption. He was a poor man, and was ill for years. An unconverted merchant in the place, who had a kind heart, used to send him now and then some things for his comfort, or for his family. He felt grateful for the kindness, but could make no return, as he wanted to do. At length he determined that the best return he could make would be to pray for the man's salvation. So he began to pray, and his soul kindled, and he got hold of God. No revival was taking place there, but, by and by, to the astonishment of everybody, this merchant came right out on the Lord's side. The fire kindled all over the place; a powerful revival followed, and multitudes were converted.

15. This poor man lingered, in this condition of weakness for several years. After his death, I visited the place, and his widow put into my hands his diary. Among other entries was this: "I am acquainted with about thirty ministers and Churches." He went then on to set apart certain hours in the day and week to pray for each of these ministers and Churches, and also certain seasons for praying for different

missionary stations. Then followed, under different dates, such facts as these: "To-day I have been enabled to offer what I call the prayer of faith for the outpouring of the Spirit on —— Church, and I trust in God there will soon be a revival there." Under another date he had written: "I have to-day been able to offer what I call the prayer of faith for —— Church, and trust there will soon be a revival there." Thus he had gone over a great number of Churches, recording the fact that he had prayed for them in faith that a revival might soon prevail among them.

Of the missionary stations, he mentioned in particular one at Ceylon. I believe the last place mentioned in his diary, for which he offered the prayer of faith, was the place in which he lived. Not long after, the revival commenced, and went over the region of country, nearly, I believe, if not quite, in the order in which the places had been mentioned in his diary; and in due time news came from Ceylon that there was a revival of religion there. The revival in his own town did not commence till after his death. Its commencement was at the time when his widow put into my hands the document to which I have refrered. She told me that he was so exercised in prayer during his sickness that she often feared he would "pray himself to death."

The revival was exceedingly great and powerful in all the region, and the fact that it was about to prevail had not been hidden from this servant of the Lord. According to His Word, "the secret of the Lord is with them that fear Him" (Ps. xxv. 14). Thus, this man, too feeble in body to go out of his house, was yet more useful to the world and the Church of God than all the heartless professors in the country.

16. If you are filled with the Spirit, you will not find yourselves distressed, and galled, and worried, when people speak against you. When I find people irritated and fretting

at any little thing that touches them, I am sure they have not been filled with the Spirit of Christ. Jesus Christ could have everything said against Him that malice could invent, and yet not be in the least disturbed by it. If you mean to be meek under persecution, and exemplify the temper of the Saviour, and honour religion in this way, you need to be filled with the Spirit.

You will be wise in using means for the conversion of sinners. If the Spirit of God is in you, He will lead you to use means wisely, in a way adapted to the end, and to avoid doing hurt.

(*Note.*—A remarkable instance of divine leading in the choice of a subject, and the management of a meeting which occurred in Finney's experience, aptly illustrates his point. In the outskirts of Antwerp, N.Y., where no religious services were usually held, he preached on the escape of Lot from Sodom. It so happened that the place was commonly called "Sodom," and the one pious man of the neighbourhood (who had invited Finney) was known as "Lot." Finney was entirely unaware of this, but the people, imagining him to have chosen the subject deliberately, in order to reproach them, were full of fury. In the end, however, there was an extraordinary breakdown, under the influence of the Spirit. Penitent sinners began to fall upon their knees in every direction, crying to God for mercy. "If I had had a sword in each hand, I could not have cut them down so fast as they fell," said Finney. The meeting continued all night, and in the morning (the building being required for school purposes) was adjourned to a private house, Finney renewing his labours in the afternoon. Years after, a minister who called upon him in order to give a donation of a hundred dollars to Oberlin College, proved to be one of the converts from that school-house meeting.)

17. You will be calm under affliction; not thrown into confusion or consternation when you see the storm coming over you. People around will be astonished at your calmness and cheerfulness under heavy trials, not knowing the inward supports of those who are filled with the Spirit.

If you have not the Spirit, you will be very apt to stumble

at those who have. You will doubt the propriety of their conduct. If they seem to feel a good deal more than yourself, you will be likely to call it "animal feeling." You will perhaps doubt their sincerity when they say they have such feelings. You will say: "I don't know what to make of Brother Such-a-one; he seems to be very pious, but I do not understand him, I think he has a great deal of animal feeling." Thus you will be trying to censure them, for the purpose of justifying yourself.

18. If you mean to have the Spirit, you must be child-like, and yield to His influences—just as yielding as air. If He is drawing you to prayer, you must quit everything to yield to His gentle strivings. No doubt you have sometimes felt a desire to pray for some object, and you have put it off and resisted, until God left you. If you wish Him to remain, you must yield to His softest leadings, watch to learn what He would have you do, and yield yourself up to His guidance.

19. Christians ought to be willing to make any sacrifice to enjoy the presence of the Spirit. Said a woman in high life (a professor of religion): "I must either give up hearing such-and-such a minister (likely Finney) preach, or I must give up my gay company." She gave up the preaching and stayed away. How different from another case—that of a woman in the same rank of life—who heard the same minister preach, and went home resolved to abandon her gay and worldly manner of life. She changed her whole mode of dress, of equipage, of living, and of conversation; so that her gay and worldly friends were soon willing to leave her to the enjoyment of communion with God, and free to spend her time in doing good.

You see from this, that it must be very difficult for those in fashionable life to go to heaven. What a calamity to be in such circles! Who can enjoy the presence of God in them?

"Wherefore the rather, brethren, give diligence to make your calling and election sure: for if ye do these things, ye shall never fall: for so an entrance shall be ministered unto you abundantly into the everlasting kingdom of our Lord and Saviour Jesus Christ" (2 Pet. i. 10–11).

# FIVE THINGS A PREACHER NEEDS

## By Rev. E. E. Shelhamer

In my private devotions I frequently pray about five needs, and if perchance others may be profited, I herewith mention them.

First, *Purity*. It is not enough to have at one time obtained the blessed experience of heart purity. No, I must meet the Lord frequently, and feel His purity surging through my being. This will imply not only purity of heart, but purity in thought and deed. When I leave a person or a home I must leave it as pure as I found it; yea, in a better shape if possible. In short, I must be clean in spirit, in person, and in contact with others—a good representative of Jesus.

Second, *Humility*. Dear Lord, let me be truly humble; so humble I will reflect Thy humility; so humble I will not be conscious that I *am* humble, and yet others will be reproved and inspired as they behold Thy gentleness in me. As Andrew Murray would say, "Let me have perfect quietness of heart, and never be fretted, or irritated, or sore, or disappointed; so that I expect nothing and wonder at nothing that is done to me, and feel no resentment at anything done against me; to feel at rest when nobody praises me and when I am blamed or despised. To have a blessed home in the Lord where I can go and shut the door, and kneel to my Father in secret, and where I am at peace as in a deep sea of calmness when all around and above is trouble."

Third, *Charity*. By charity I mean that I want to be so magnanimous that I will put the best construction on the deeds of others; saved from a critical spirit so that the reputation of others will be safe in my hands. Lord, forbid that I should find it easy when preaching, or in conversation, to go out of my way and cast a reflection upon another when he is not able to explain. Let me always practise the Golden Rule and "do unto others as I would that they should do unto me."

Fourth, *Chastity*. I want to be so chaste that anything which savours of coarseness and suggestiveness will have no place in me. I must not shock the most refined with anything that borders on looseness and rudeness. Let me never use language or gestures in the pulpit which tend to cheapen the gospel of the Son of God.

Fifth, *Brevity*. Let me know when and how to quit. I fear that I sometimes preach people under conviction, than preach it off. Better not finish my sermon and have a fruitful appeal, than preach ten minutes too long and lose one seeker. More than once have I started in the spirit, and I fear ended in the flesh. In other words, I reached a climax and failed quickly to draw the net: some of the fish escaped. What a pity! Lord, have mercy! Once more I plead for Purity, Humility, Charity, Chastity, and Brevity.

## FÉLIX-ANTOINE SAVARD

Félix-Antoine Savard, né à Québec en 1896, fait ses études classiques et théologiques au Petit puis au Grand Séminaire de Chicoutimi. Ordonné prêtre en 1922, il est d'abord professeur de rhétorique. Il débute ensuite, à Bagotville, un long ministère qui le conduit auprès des hommes de bois de la région de Charlevoix. C'est là qu'il rencontre le maître-draveur Joseph Boies, le modèle de Menaud. Vicaire à La Malbaie, puis curé de Clermont, il fonde aussi deux paroisses en Abitibi où il est prêtre colonisateur. Il publie *Menaud, maître-draveur*, en 1937, couronné par le Prix de l'Académie française et le Prix de la Province de Québec. Suivront d'autres œuvres, tant romanesques et dramatiques que poétiques et intimistes. En 1944, il fonde avec Luc Lacourcière les Archives de folklore de l'Université Laval, où il sera doyen de la Faculté des lettres de 1950 à 1957. Il se retire dans la région de Charlevoix à la fin des années 1960. Le Prix Athanase-David lui est attribué en 1968 pour l'ensemble de son œuvre. Il s'éteint à Québec le 23 août 1982.

## MENAUD, MAÎTRE-DRAVEUR

Ce roman de F.-A. Savard est un classique de la littérature québécoise. Il raconte la lutte du vieux Menaud pour délivrer son peuple de l'asservissement des étrangers, entendons des Anglais, qui se sont emparés de la Montagne, microcosme du pays. On assiste à la mort de Joson, fils unique de Menaud, emporté par la débâcle. Menaud, rongé par la douleur, tente de rallier à sa cause les habitants de Mainsal. Seul le Lucon, son fils spirituel, accepte de le suivre et d'affronter le Délié, le traître, dans un combat qui est loin de tourner à son avantage. À son tour, Menaud voudra affronter le traître. Perdu dans la tempête, mais sauvé par le Lucon, Menaud sombre dans la folie. L'action du maître-draveur n'aura cependant pas été inutile. Le Lucon et Marie, fille de Menaud, sont déterminés à poursuivre la lutte.